engage

C000071504

Who is Jesus? Does prayer r
suffering in the world? Is it OK to date non-Christians? What
is a Leviathan? What does church actually do? What does
true wisdom look like? What's another word for thesaurus?
We'll tackle most of these questions in engage 17.

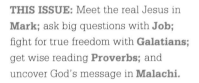

✱ DAILY READINGS Each day's
page throws you into the Bible, to
get you handling, questioning and
exploring God's message to you —
encouraging you to act on it and talk
to God more in prayer.

THIS ISSUE: Meet the real Jesus in
Mark; ask big questions with **Job;**
fight for true freedom with **Galatians;**
get wise reading **Proverbs;** and
uncover God's message in **Malachi.**

✱ TAKE IT FURTHER If you're
hungry for more at the end of an
engage page, turn to the **Take it
further** section to dig deeper.

✱ TRICKY tackles those mind-
bendingly tricky questions that
confuse us all, as well as questions
our friends bombard us with.
This time we ask: **Does prayer
really work?**

✱ STUFF Articles on stuff relevant
to the lives of young Christians. This
issue we focus on **relationships.**

✱ REAL LIVES True stories,
revealing God at work in people's
lives. This time — **the life and
death of a missionary.**

✱ TOOLBOX is full of tools to help
you understand the Bible. This issue
we look at the **timeline of the Bible.**

✱ ESSENTIAL Articles on the
basics we really need to know about
God, the Bible and Christianity.
This issue, we find out exactly what
church does.

**All of us who work on engage are
passionate to see the Bible at
work in people's lives. Do you
want God's word to have an
impact on your life? Then open
your Bible, and start on the first
engage study right now...**

HOW TO USE engage

1 Set a time you can read the Bible every day

2 Find a place where you can be quiet and think

3 Grab your Bible, pen and a notebook

4 Ask God to help you understand what you read

5 Read the day's verses with **engage,** taking time to think about it

6 Pray about what you've read

BIBLE STUFF We use the NIV Bible version, so you might find it's the best one to use with **engage**. If the notes say **"Read Mark 1 v 1–8"**, look up Mark in the contents page at the front of your Bible. It'll tell you which page Mark starts on. Find chapter 1 of Mark, and then verse 1 of chapter 1 (the verse numbers are the tiny ones). Then start reading. Simple.

In this issue...

ENGAGE 17 CONTRIBUTORS AND THEIR FAVE BOARDGAMES:

Writers: Martin Cole (Hungry Hippos) Cassie Martin (Twister) Carl Laferton (Risk)
Jim Overton (Chess) Helen Thorne (Snakes & Ladders)
Designer: Steve Devane (Absolute Balderdash)
Proof-readers: Anne Woodcock (Formula One) Nicole Carter (Cluedo/Clue)
Editor: Martin Cole (say hello to us — martin@thegoodbook.co.uk)

Mark

Guess who

Have you ever played the game Guess Who? You know the one — "Does yours have a moustache?"

"Nope, is yours wearing a hat?"

As you narrow down the options, you finally work out who is on the other person's card.

Well, the early part of Mark's Gospel is a bit like Guess Who. At least, it is for the disciples. They spend the first eight chapters trying to figure out exactly who Jesus is. Look out for the number of times people are amazed and confused in these early chapters.

It's slightly easier for us — Mark starts his whole Gospel with a very big hint. Check out verse 1: *"The beginning of the gospel about Jesus Christ, the Son of God."*

"Gospel" of course means "good "news", and as somebody once said: "If you don't think the good news about Jesus is the best thing you've

ever heard, you can be sure you haven't really understood it."

We see why Jesus is such good news as we start to understand what He is like. God in human flesh, walking on earth and stepping into history. He shows us what God is like — His power and compassion as He defeats evil and brings healing and forgiveness. He even invites us into His amazing kingdom!

Who is this man?

Jesus Christ, the Son of God. He's finally here and that's not just good news; it's great news!

1 ┆ Get ready!

Mark's story of Jesus is fast-paced. It's like a film with scene changes every few verses. He's got some great news to share and he's not going to get bogged down with loads of description. So let's not hang around...

👁 Read Mark 1 v 1

Jesus means "God saves". *Christ* means "God's chosen King" and *the Son of God* is self-explanatory.

👁 Read verses 2–8

ENGAGE YOUR BRAIN

▷ Who is the quote from Isaiah talking about?

▷ Who is he preparing the way for?

Stop for a minute and let that really sink in. Hundreds of years before Jesus' birth, Isaiah dropped a huge bombshell. God Himself would come. To earth. In person. And now it's happening — John the Baptist is the messenger announcing the King's imminent arrival.

▷ What does John say is the first step towards forgiveness? (v4)

It's pretty difficult to forgive someone who doesn't think they've done anything wrong. Repentance —

recognising and turning away from your sin — is an important first step.

▷ What do you make of John's interesting fashion and diet choices? (v6)

John was basically following the prophet dress code from the Old Testament. He was the last prophet before Jesus — God's final, perfect word to humanity — arrived.

PRAY ABOUT IT

Thank God for sending His Son to us. Tell Him what that means to you.

THE BOTTOM LINE

Jesus is good news!

→ TAKE IT FURTHER

Are you ready for more? Try p110.

2 | Baptism, blessing & temptation

There's a lot going on in these four verses as we see Jesus for the first time. But His first appearance doesn't just come out of nowhere — it has been hinted at through the whole Old Testament.

👁 Read Mark 1 v 9–13

ENGAGE YOUR BRAIN

▶ List the things that happen when Jesus is baptised:

•

•

•

▶ What do we learn about Jesus?

We get an amazing insight into Jesus' status as the eternally loved Son of God. Here, God the Father confirms who Jesus is and His delight in Him. The Holy Spirit (the third member of the Trinity) is also involved in blessing this mission as Jesus begins His rescue of humanity.

▶ What happens to Jesus next? (v12–13)

▶ Can you think of any other events that took place in the desert, related to the number 40?

When God rescued His people from slavery in Egypt (see the book of Exodus), they wandered around in the desert for 40 years because they gave in to temptation and put God to the test. Jesus' time in the desert shows Him resisting temptation and being the perfectly obedient Son that Israel never was.

PRAY ABOUT IT

Thank God that Jesus is His perfect Son, who came to rescue us and who was perfectly qualified to do so, never sinning or failing as we do.

THE BOTTOM LINE

Jesus is perfectly qualified to rescue us.

→ TAKE IT FURTHER
Flutter over to page 110.

3 | Here comes the kingdom

Now we hear Jesus speak for the first time in Mark's Gospel — what will He say? What is His agenda going to be? What effect will it have?

👁 Read Mark 1 v 14–15

ENGAGE YOUR BRAIN

▷ *What is Jesus' message? (v15)*

God's plan to rescue the world, which was planned before the world was even created, is about to take place. The "kingdom of God" means God ruling over His people. The kingdom is near because the King has arrived, and the way in is to turn from sin and accept the good news of Jesus' rescue.

👁 Read verses 16–20

▷ *What does Jesus say to these fishermen? (v16–20)*

▷ *How do they respond?*

▷ *Is this surprising?*

▷ *What do they leave behind?*

▷ *What do you think Jesus means in v17?*

It's a massive thing to suddenly leave everything — family, friends, job and home — just because a stranger tells you to. But Jesus has the authority to demand that. He's not necessarily asking us to leave home but He's still asking us to follow Him today.

GET ON WITH IT

▷ *Have you answered Jesus' call?*

▷ *Are you following Him?*

▷ *Is He more important than your friends, family, career or possessions?*

▷ *Do you know what it means to repent and believe the good news and have you experienced that in your own life?*

PRAY ABOUT IT

Talk to God honestly about your answers.

→ TAKE IT FURTHER

Kingdom come — page 110.

4 | The Holy One of God

We see more examples of Jesus' extraordinary authority now as He teaches, heals and casts out evil spirits. Prepare to be amazed...

👁 Read Mark 1 v 21–34

ENGAGE YOUR BRAIN
▷ *What is so unusual about Jesus' teaching? (v22)*

Jesus was more impressive than the teachers of the law. They would back up their teaching from the Old Testament, just as we look to the Bible. But Jesus' authority comes from Himself — God inspired the scriptures in the first place!

▷ *What does the unclean spirit recognise about Jesus? (v24)*

▷ *How does Jesus deal with it?*

▷ *How do the people around react? (v27–28)*

▷ *What is the next thing Jesus does?*

▷ *What does it show about Him? (v29–31)*

▷ *What is Simon's mother-in-law's reaction? (v31)*

▷ *What else does Jesus do? What does this show us? (v32–34)*

All these miracles point to the sort of kingdom this King is bringing — one without evil or sickness.

PRAY ABOUT IT
Thank God that we have such a powerful and compassionate King in Jesus. Pray that you would listen to His teaching and obey it because He is the ultimate authority.

THE BOTTOM LINE
Jesus is the ultimate authority.

→ TAKE IT FURTHER
Want some more? Try page 110.

5 Miracle man

The news is spreading – Jesus is something special, even if people aren't quite sure what that means yet. But right now, He needs some time alone to focus on His real priorities.

👁 **Read Mark 1 v 35–45**

ENGAGE YOUR BRAIN

▶ What does Jesus do in v35?

▶ What does this show about how important prayer is to Him?

▶ How important is it to you to spend time talking to your Heavenly Father?

PRAY ABOUT IT

Ask God to give you the same desire for spending time talking to Him that Jesus had. Prayer can be hard — we need God's Spirit to help us.

▶ When the disciples find Him, what does Jesus say is His priority?

▶ Does this surprise you? Do you really see preaching as the main reason He came?

▶ How does that affect how you listen to Jesus' words in the Bible?

Despite his main priority, Jesus still has time for individuals.

▶ What does He do for the man with leprosy? (v41–42)

According to Old Testament law, touching an unclean person like this leper would make you unclean. But Jesus is so holy that instead His cleanness transfers over to the unclean leper!

▶ Can you think of another way in which Jesus will do that for unclean/sinful people?

Check out Acts 10 v 36–43.

PRAY ABOUT IT

Now use those powerful verses as you talk to God.

→ **TAKE IT FURTHER**

Shhh! Keep quiet and go to page 111.

6 | Raising the roof

What is your greatest need? For the starving it might seem like food; the lonely might say relationship. Your answer is probably driven by your circumstances. But Jesus has a very different take on things.

👁 **Read Mark 2 v 1–5**

ENGAGE YOUR BRAIN

▷ Just how popular is Jesus? (v1–2)

▷ How desperate are the men with the paralysed friend? (v4)

▷ Why is Jesus' response to them so surprising? (v5)

▷ What do they expect Him to do?

Being sinful and unforgiven is such a bad situation that it makes being paralysed seem like a minor issue!

👁 **Read verses 6–12**

▷ Why are the teachers of the law so outraged? (v6–7)

▷ Are they right?

Only God can forgive sins. Only the wronged person can offer forgiveness. As all sin is ultimately against God, only He can forgive it.

▷ So what's Jesus claiming?

▷ How would you answer Jesus' question in v9?

On one hand it seems harder to heal someone than merely say: "Your sins are forgiven". But real forgiveness is much harder. It was so difficult and costly that it led Jesus to the cross.

▷ How does Jesus prove His authority? (v10–11)

▷ What's the reaction? (v12)

PRAY ABOUT IT

"Forgive us our sins" says the Lord's Prayer. Have you asked for God's forgiveness today and thanked Him that it is possible through Jesus' death and resurrection?

THE BOTTOM LINE

Jesus can forgive our sins!

➔ **TAKE IT FURTHER**

Grab some more on page 111.

7 Sin sickness

When someone is diagnosed with a life-threatening illness, their immediate reaction can often be denial — refusing to accept reality. But that's a dangerous place to be when it comes to our spiritual health.

👁 Read Mark 2 v 13–17

ENGAGE YOUR BRAIN

▶ Who is the surprise choice for new disciple? (v14)

If you tell someone you work for the tax office these days it might go down like a brick in water. Back in Jesus' day it meant you were collaborating with the enemy occupiers (the Romans) and probably squeezing more money out of people than you were entitled too. Tax collector = traitor and crook.

▶ Who is Jesus spending time with? (v15)

▶ What is the reaction of the religious and "respectable" people? (v16)

▶ Have they got a point?

▶ How does Jesus explain his actions? (v17)

The "sinners" and tax collectors had a huge advantage over the "religious" people. They knew they needed God's mercy and forgiveness. To use Jesus' metaphor, they knew they were sick and needed a doctor.

The irony is that everyone is sick and needs a doctor. But many people are in denial and think they're good enough for God. They don't think they're sick and so won't turn to Jesus for help. It's a dangerous place to be.

PRAY ABOUT IT

Have you admitted your need of Jesus' forgiveness? Do you judge people who seem to be worse "sinners" than you? Ask God to help you see people the way Jesus does.

THE BOTTOM LINE

Jesus came for sinners.

→ TAKE IT FURTHER

More treatment on page 111.

8 Fast and furious

What do you think a "religious" or "spiritual" person should be like? Think about it for a moment and then let's see if Jesus fits your description.

👁 Read Mark 2 v 18–20

ENGAGE YOUR BRAIN

Going without food for a time to concentrate on prayer was often a way of showing sorrow and repentance for sin.

▷ *Why does Jesus say this is inappropriate for His followers? (v19–20)*

You don't generally choose to mourn and go without food at a wedding — it's a celebration! Jesus' presence (remember He's the King) brings great joy to His followers. But notice the hint, even early on in Mark's Gospel, that sad times are coming (v20).

👁 Read verses 21–22

▷ *What point do you think Jesus is making about old ways of relating to God and how His coming changes things? (v21–22)*

You couldn't just slot Jesus and His message into the Jewish religion.

He'd come to do something that, while fulfilling the Old Testament, was radically new. And He was its focus.

PRAY ABOUT IT

One of the characteristics of a Christian is joy. Even when circumstances are hard, we can have great joy because we know and love the King and are known and loved by Him. Ask God to help you to know that joy and to share it with people around you.

THE BOTTOM LINE

Jesus is our joy!

→ TAKE IT FURTHER

Go to page 111... fast!

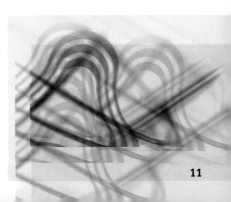

9 | An ear for trouble

Mark has been revealing Jesus to us. So far, no one around Jesus has really worked out who He is. The religious leaders were the blindest of all. Let's see them completely miss the point again.

👁 Read Mark 2 v 23–28

ENGAGE YOUR BRAIN

▶ What was the Sabbath all about in Jewish life? (Check out Exodus 20 v 8–11)

▶ What was Jesus being criticised for? (v23–24)

By Jesus' day the command not to work on the Sabbath had been so twisted that even the disciples picking a few ears of corn to eat was classified as work. According to the Pharisees, they were breaking the Sabbath and sinning.

▶ How does Jesus deal with this accusation? (v25–26)

▶ What does Jesus point out about the purpose of the Sabbath? (v27)

▶ Why do you think we find it easier to think God is trying to spoil our fun than care for us?

▶ What does Jesus claim about Himself? (v28)

God gave the Sabbath to His people for their benefit, not to make life harder for them. The religious leaders had missed the point again. But more amazingly than that, Jesus is Lord of the Sabbath — He created the Sabbath and He's the one who gives perfect rest.

SHARE IT

When you're chatting with friends, how can you dispel the myth that God is out to spoil our fun?

PRAY ABOUT IT

Thank God for sending His Son, Jesus. Ask Him to help you follow Jesus with your whole life, rather than just trying to keep the rules.

THE BOTTOM LINE

We find true rest in Jesus.

→ TAKE IT FURTHER

More wise words on page 111.

10 | Withered religion

**More Sabbath shenanigans today, as we see
just how wrong Jesus' enemies have got things.**

Read Mark 3 v 1–6

ENGAGE YOUR BRAIN

▷ What are Jesus' enemies waiting for? (v2)

▷ What does that show us about their hearts? Are they really interested in the suffering man?

▷ Do you think they genuinely care about honouring the Sabbath either?

▷ What does Jesus ask them? (v4)

▷ What do you think the answer is?

Resting on the Sabbath should remind God's people that they are holy like Him (Ezekiel 20 v 12). According to the religious leaders, even healing someone on the Sabbath counted as work and was breaking God's law. But they'd totally missed the point. How can it be wrong to heal someone, to show compassion?

▷ Why do you think the Pharisees are so threatened by Jesus?

Jesus is always the sworn enemy of religion. Religion says: "Do this, obey these rules and you can be right with God". Jesus says: "I've already done it. Now live in relationship with me and I will help you."

PRAY ABOUT IT

Are you falling into the trap of religion rather than relationship? Talk to God about that now, saying sorry where you need to and asking for Jesus' help to trust in Him daily.

THE BOTTOM LINE

Christianity is relationship with Jesus, not religion.

→ TAKE IT FURTHER

A little bit more is on page 111.

13

11 Jesus vs evil

Jesus faces a lot of opposition in chapter three of Mark's Gospel. We've already seen the Pharisees and Herodians plotting His death and now we see more obvious spiritual opposition.

👁 Read Mark 3 v 7–12

ENGAGE YOUR BRAIN

▶ *Where are people coming from to hear Jesus?*

If you have a map at the back of your Bible, check out the distances. Jesus' fame is spreading and people are walking huge distances to hear Him.

▶ *What does Jesus do for these crowds? (v10)*

▶ *What else happens? (v11)*

▶ *What do the evil (or impure) spirits recognise?*

👁 Read verses 13–19

▶ *What are the twelve apostles (the word means "sent ones") to do? (v14–15)*

Their message was the same one Jesus taught (Mark 1 v 15) — the kingdom of God is near; repent and believe the good news! When the

King comes, His enemies will be destroyed. That's why the apostles were given authority to cast out demons.

THINK IT OVER

Look at the world around you. Can you think of ways in which evil seems to flourish?

PRAY ABOUT IT

Thank God that Jesus defeated evil on the cross and will destroy it for ever when He returns. Thank Him that He will usher in a new world, which is the home of righteousness (2 Peter 3 v 13). Use Revelation 21 v 22 — 22 v 5 to focus your prayers.

THE BOTTOM LINE

Jesus came to destroy evil.

→ TAKE IT FURTHER

Stuff about spiritual enemies is on page 111.

12 | Jesus vs Satan

Yeah, you guessed it — Jesus faces more opposition now. Not only from the self-serving religious leaders, but from His own family too!

👁 **Read Mark 3 v 20–30**

ENGAGE YOUR BRAIN

▶ *How chaotic are the crowds getting now? (v20)*

▶ *How does His family respond to Jesus? (v21)*

▶ *How must that have felt for Jesus?*

▶ *What do the teachers of the Law accuse Him of? (v22)*

Crazy or demon-possessed. Charming. Jesus is facing opposition on all sides, and what for? Healing and casting out evil.

▶ *How does Jesus answer the teachers of the law? (v23–27)*

It's only logical. You can't fight fire with fire; you'll just end up with more fire! Jesus can only cast out evil because He is good.

▶ *What warning does Jesus give His opponents? (v28–30)*

▶ *How have they blasphemed? (v30)*

If you call good "evil", how can you ever be saved? If you reject Jesus, He can't save you. By saying that Jesus had an evil spirit rather than recognising Him as God's Son, these people are rejecting the only one who can save and forgive them.

SHARE IT

Do your friends and family know that Jesus forgives all our sins — however terrible or secret, if we'd only turn to Him?

THE BOTTOM LINE

Only Jesus can forgive us.

→ **TAKE IT FURTHER**

More about tricky v29 on page 112.

13 | The in crowd

Jesus' family still don't get it. They're concerned He's gone crazy and want to take Him home. But once again Jesus turns everything on its head.

👁 Read Mark 3 v 31–35

ENGAGE YOUR BRAIN

▶ *Who is demanding Jesus' attention? (v31–32)*

▶ *How might we expect Jesus to respond?*

Remind yourself of the sort of people Jesus is surrounded by (2 v 16).

▶ *Why are verses 33–34 such a shock?*

This whole section of Mark turns our expectations on their head. The people you would expect to be "on the inside" with Jesus — the religious leaders and even His own family — are "out". Yet the "sinners" and ordinary crowds of people, even tax collectors like Matthew are "in".

▶ *What criteria does Jesus use for admitting people into His true family? (v35)*

▶ *What do you think that means?*

This is awesome stuff. Jesus wasn't rejecting His mother and brothers; He was making a much much bigger point about responding to His teaching. People who receive it obediently are on the same level as Jesus' family! Accepting Jesus, repenting of your sin and being forgiven by Him brings you into His family. Christians are close to Jesus. Very close.

PRAY AND SHARE

▶ *Are you excited? What will you say to God?*

▶ *And what will you say to your friends who are on the outside?*

THE BOTTOM LINE

Christians are members of Jesus' family.

→ TAKE IT FURTHER

Family matters on page 112.

14 Inside out

Jesus healed people, drove out demons and wowed the crowds with His incredible teaching. Many people followed Him, yet others ignored Him or even plotted to kill Him.

👁 **Read Mark 4 v 1–12**

ENGAGE YOUR BRAIN

▶ *What does v1 remind us about the current situation?*

A parable is a simple story that teaches a big point.

▶ *What do you think is the point of this parable?*

▶ *What does Jesus say about parables? (v10–12)*

▶ *Does that surprise you?*

Jesus quotes Isaiah 6 v 9–10 in verse 12. Isaiah's job was to preach about God's judgment to the nation of Israel, but here's the kicker — he was to use parables so they wouldn't understand or repent. Pretty harsh? Yep, but it was all part of God's judgment on their constant sin.

▶ *What does Jesus say to the disciples? (v11)*

▶ *How is this different to what Isaiah was told to do?*

▶ *Did you spot the inside/outside distinction again?*

▶ *What makes someone an insider/ outsider? (v11)*

PRAY ABOUT IT
As always in His dealings with humanity, it's all about God's grace. We can't understand or even begin to repent unless God makes it clear to us. Thank God that Jesus came to do just that and still does today. Pray for God's grace in the lives of your friends or family who don't yet know Him.

THE BOTTOM LINE
Jesus brings outsiders in.

→ TAKE IT FURTHER
Understand this: turn to page 112.

Tomorrow: Jesus explains the parable.

15 | Gone to seed

Remember the parable of the sower/seeds/soil?
Now we get the explanation...

Read Mark 4 v 13–20

ENGAGE YOUR BRAIN

▶ What is the seed (v14)?

▶ Look back at verses 3-8 and then fill in the grid below:

Where the seed landed	What happened to it?	What does it mean?

▶ What are the two basic reactions to God's word?

PRAY ABOUT IT

If we have accepted the word of the gospel and are living fruitful,
transformed lives, then we're the good soil. But are you ever like the
bad soil — easily distracted, tempted away or discouraged when things
get tough? Pray now that God would make you good soil and that
God's word would put down deep roots in your life.

GET ON WITH IT

The Sower/Farmer sowed the seed widely, scattering it everywhere. Do you
do that? Do you share the good news about Jesus with anyone and everyone?

→ TAKE IT FURTHER How to suck seed on page 112.

16 See hear

So if we're the good soil, what does that look like — how can we be fruitful for God?

👁 Read Mark 4 v 21–25

ENGAGE YOUR BRAIN

- ▶ What is Jesus' main point in v21–23?
- ▶ What do you think the light represents in v21?
- ▶ How do v11 and v34 help us to understand?

Jesus is talking about displaying and sharing something wonderful. In this case He's probably referring to His teaching about God's Kingdom.

- ▶ How should we respond to Jesus' word? (v23)
- ▶ Have you?
- ▶ What does Jesus say we should do with the light (His message) in v21?
- ▶ What do you think that means for you?

GET ON WITH IT

- ▶ Do you keep the good news about Jesus to yourself?
- ▶ How can you change (with God's help) today?

THINK IT OVER

- ▶ How should we respond to God's word (v24)?
- ▶ Do you do that? Or do you shut your Bible and forget about it 5 minutes later?
- ▶ What's the promise for those who take God's word seriously? (v25)
- ▶ What is the warning for those who don't?

Some of those listening to Jesus would have considered His words carefully: not understanding it all but wanting to and asking Him to explain, like the disciples. Others didn't really listen or take it to heart.

PRAY ABOUT IT

Pray that you would be like the first sort of person and that God would make you fruitful in your faith (v20).

THE BOTTOM LINE

Listen to Jesus and share His message.

→ TAKE IT FURTHER

Listen up — go to page 112.

17 | Ready, steady, grow!

More parables, this time giving us an insight into God's kingdom, of which Jesus is the King. If you're starting to think this is all very familiar, listen up — the first parable appears only in Mark's Gospel. It's a rarity.

👁 Read Mark 4 v 26–34

ENGAGE YOUR BRAIN

▶ *What is the kingdom of God like?*
v26–29:
v30–32:

▶ *How does God's kingdom arrive and grow?*

▶ *Would this be surprising for His original listeners? What might they have expected?*

▶ *When we look at the world around us, does it seem as if God's kingdom has come?*

Your church, CU or youth group might seem fairly insignificant. Maybe it's large and flourishing. Or maybe you're one of only two or three teenagers in a cold, half-empty building every Sunday and the "kingdom of God" looks unimpressive to say the least.

But Jesus says this is what you should expect — it looks small now (like the mustard seed) but its growth is supernatural — it's down to God and one day it will be seen by everyone.

THINK IT OVER

Look at the world around you again. Any signs that God's kingdom has come and is growing? Look carefully!

PRAY ABOUT IT

Ask God to help you see His kingdom and to have faith when appearances are deceptive. Thank Him that one day His church will give Him great glory and be seen to do so by the whole world.

THE BOTTOM LINE

The kingdom of God starts small... but ends huge.

→ TAKE IT FURTHER

Check out another view on page 113.

18 | That sinking feeling

What sorts of things frighten you? Spiders? Horror movies? Going to the dentist? We see some genuine fear in these next verses, and an amazing response to that fear.

👁 **Read Mark 4 v 35–41**

ENGAGE YOUR BRAIN

🔹 *Again, how many people are following Jesus? (v36)*
🔹 *What natural event blows up? (v37)*
🔹 *What is the disciples' reaction (remember at least 4 of them were experienced fishermen)?*
🔹 *What makes this situation seem hopeless? (v37–38)*
🔹 *What does Jesus do? (v39)*
🔹 *What is the result? Why is this miracle so amazing?*

Even when a storm has blown over, it takes ages for the waves to die down. Not this time. Apparently the words Jesus uses in v39 are the sort of thing you might say to a boisterous family pet. All He has to do is speak and all is totally calm. Remember how God made the world?

🔹 *Have we seen Jesus show his power and authority like this before in Mark?*

🔹 *Do the disciples recognise who Jesus is yet?*

👁 **Read Psalm 89 v 8–9**

🔹 *Who is Jesus?*
🔹 *How should the disciples have responded? (v40)*
🔹 *What hadn't they realised yet? (v41)*

PRAY ABOUT IT

Thank Jesus that He has authority over sickness, evil, natural disasters and even death (see chapter 5). Thank Him that when He returns, His new world will have none of those things in it.

THE BOTTOM LINE

Jesus is in total control.

→ **TAKE IT FURTHER**

Sail on to page 113.

Does prayer really work?

Each issue in TRICKY, we tackle those mind-bendingly difficult questions that confuse us all, as well as questions that friends bombard us with to catch us off guard.
This time we ask: Is there any point in praying?
Does God actually listen to us?

WHY BOTHER PRAYING?

In the Bible, God is very clear — He expects His people to pray. Again and again He instructs us to talk to Him.

"Devote yourselves to prayer, being watchful and thankful" (Colossians 4 v 2).

"And pray in the Spirit on all occasions with all kinds of prayers and requests. With this in mind, be alert and always keep on praying for all the saints" (Ephesians 6 v 18).

God doesn't want us to talk to Him because He's lonely (don't flatter yourself!). It's a huge part of your relationship with Him. Praying helps you remember, trust in and enjoy God's forgiveness (Matthew 6 v 12). You gain spiritual strength through prayer (Ephesians 3 v 16–19). You're

equipped to resist temptation through prayer (Luke 22 v 40). Prayer is vital in sharing the gospel (Colossians 4 v 3). Prayer can play a part in physical healing (James 5 v 14–15).

But does prayer actually work?

PRAYER CHANGES THINGS

In the Bible, there are loads of examples of prayer changing things. God was going to wipe out the Israelites for worshipping the golden calf, but Moses prayed for them to be spared and God didn't kill them (Deuteronomy 9 v 7–19). Hannah couldn't get pregnant and prayed like crazy for a son. She later gave birth to Samuel, whose name means "heard by God" (1 Samuel 1 v 1–20).

Jonah offered a panic prayer while in the big fish's stomach. God heard him

and caused the fish to spew Jonah up onto the beach (Jonah 2 v 7–10). There are many many more examples of God answering prayer in the Bible. Talk to Christians and they'll tell you of brilliant instances in their lives too.

TALKING TO GOD

We can talk to God and tell Him what's on our minds. In your situation, you might be asking God to give you a new job, smooth out relationship problems, cure an illness, fix family problems, sort out financial difficulties, or something else. God can and does answer prayers like these. Sometimes His answers to prayer are "Yes", sometimes "No", and sometimes "Wait".

He loves to hear us talk to Him about anything. Never think that a problem is too big for God to handle, or too small to care about. Notice that Jesus didn't put any limits on the types of requests we can bring to God: *"Ask and it will be given to you; seek and you will find; knock and the door will be opened to you"* (Matthew 7 v 7).

PRAYER CHANGES YOU

Get ready for things to happen when you pray. Prayer changes things. But most of all, be prepared for your prayers to change **you**. Talking with God takes you out of your humdrum world and connects you with the Creator of the universe. When you pray, you are immediately in God's presence.

Prayer also changes your attitude and focus. Let's admit it, we all tend to be self-centred, even when praying. But our prayers should focus on who God is and what He wants to accomplish in our lives. As we pray sincerely, we begin to align ourselves with God's plans rather than our own. In our prayers, we make God the focal point of our life, so we change from being self-centred to being God centred.

Prayer does work, God does listen to us and it will change your life. So what are you waiting for?

Ideas taken from "Talking with God" by Bruce Bickel and Stan Jantz, published by Harvest House.

Job

Why me?

The young boy gets mercilessly picked on at school. He cries all the way home and sobs into his pillow. Why is life like this?

Cancer strikes a young mother. A happy personality is turned into a devastated shadow of her former self. The fear is crippling too. Why did this happen?

The teenager never felt more lonely in a crowd. She'd never go to a party again. Not now she was in a wheelchair. Why is it like this?

Why do bad things happen to good people? And why do Christians sometimes seem to get a double dose? Doesn't God care? Or is He powerless to do anything about it?

The book of Job doesn't provide any quick or easy answers to the problem of suffering. But it does lead us to God. And it's only in the awesome presence of God that we can begin to get a right view on life's hardships.

We'll stay with Job every step of his harrowing journey. From happy highs to miserable, painful lows. Through loss, sickness and unexplained suffering. We'll see him ask: "Why me?" We'll stand back amazed at his friends' response. We'll even discover what true wisdom is. And then we'll see the Lord answer Job and we'll bow down to His power and perfection.

Job is like no other book you'll read. It's heavy going but so rewarding. Stay the distance and see God pulling you into a more real relationship with Him.

19 ¦ Satan's takeaway ¦

Job is famous for being a man who went through times of incredible suffering. But life wasn't always bleak for him. Let's start at the beginning...

👁 Read Job 1 v 1–5

ENGAGE YOUR BRAIN

▷ *What did Job have going for him?*
v1:
v2–3:

Job was rich. But more importantly, he was close to God. He was so determined to live right for God that he made sure every possible sin of his children was forgiven (v5).

👁 Read verses 6–12

▷ *What was God's view of Job? (v8)*

▷ *What did Satan claim was the reason for Job being godly? (v10)*

▷ *What did God allow Satan to do? (v12)*

▷ *What limits did he put on Satan?*

Verse 9 is a key to the book — is Job only godly because God's given him loads of good things? See what's at stake? God's honour. Satan's

suggesting: "People only trust you, God, when you bless them. It seems you have to buy people's allegiance."

👁 Read verses 13–22

▷ *What did Job lose?*

▷ *What's surprising about Job's response? (v20–22)*

No blame. No wallowing in self-pity. Job knew God had the right to do anything with him. It's a hard lesson to learn: God made us and is in charge of everything. He has every right to take things away from us.

PRAY ABOUT IT

Think about why you live God's way, and talk to Him about it. Thank Him for all He's given you. If you truly mean it, ask God to do whatever He wishes with everything you have. To use your life, talents and possessions for His glory.

→ TAKE IT FURTHER

More Satan stuff on page 113.

20 | A sore point

Satan wanted to prove that people only loved God when God gave the good stuff. So Job lost his wealth and his children, yet he still didn't turn against God. But Satan hadn't finished with Job.

Read Job 2 v 1–10

ENGAGE YOUR BRAIN

- What did Satan think would turn Job against God? (v4–5)

- How bad was it? (v7–8)

- What did Job's wife think he should do? (v9)

- What point did Job make? (v10)

Satan wouldn't accept defeat and continued to attack Job. All Job could do was sit in mourning, scraping at his horrible sores. Disgusting. Even his wife thought he should give up, blame God and wait for death. Job couldn't see why these disasters had happened, but he refused to blame God. As Job rightly said, we can't accept good times from God but not bad times too.

THINK IT OVER

- Do you ever blame God when bad things happen?

- Do you thank Him enough for the good things He gives you?

Talk to God about these issues now.

Read verses 11–13

- How did Job's friends react?
  v11:
  v12:
  v13:

This may not seem much, but this week-long silence was the best support they gave Job. Everything they said would undo this good work.

GET ON WITH IT

- Who do you know who's suffering?

- How will you show sympathy and support to them?

Ask God to comfort them and to help you be a good friend to them.

→ TAKE IT FURTHER

Silent sympathy on page 113.

21 | Happy deathday!

"I wish I'd never been born!" "It would be better if I were dead." Ever heard someone say that kind of thing? Maybe you've felt like that yourself. Well, that's exactly the way Job was feeling and he wasn't ashamed to say it.

👁 Read Job 3 v 1–26

ENGAGE YOUR BRAIN

▶ *What kind of questions did Job ask God?*

▶ *Why does he think dying in the womb would have been better? (v13, 17)*

▶ *How does death compare to Job's current situation? (v26)*

Job was in so much pain and misery he wished his birthday was wiped from the calendar. That way he would never have been born, so he couldn't experience all this pain. He even wished a huge sea monster — Leviathan — would swallow his day of birth!

Let's face it, Job was far from satisfied, but he still refused to turn his back on God. Instead, in brutal honesty, he took all his difficult and indignant questions to God.

THINK IT OVER

▶ *When life kicks you in the gut, do you sulk and blame God, or talk to Him about it?*

▶ *What in your life right now do you need to talk to God about?*

PRAY ABOUT IT

It's OK to take your troubles to God. Tell Him all about them. You can be miserable with Him!

Be honest with God right now. Tell Him how you feel. Tell Him what's getting you down or troubling you. Ask Him to help you trust Him through tough times. And thank Him for good things in your life too!

THE BOTTOM LINE

Take your troubles to God.

→ TAKE IT FURTHER

Thorny issues on page 113.

22 : The silence is over

When Job's friends heard of the tragedy in his life, they came to comfort him. They sat in silence with Job for a week. But now they're bursting with things to say to him. First up is Eliphaz.

👁 Read Job 4 v 1–11

▶ *How does Eliphaz describe Job's situation? (v3–5)*

▶ *Why does he think Job should have hope? (v6)*

▶ *What big point does he make in v7–9?*

▶ *Do you agree with it?*

👁 Read verses 12–21

▶ *Where did Eliphaz claim his advice came from? (v12–16)*

Eliphaz said that God doesn't punish innocent people. So Job must have sinned since he was suffering so much. Eliphaz even claimed his advice was given to him in a vision, so surely he must be right. But Eliphaz was wrong. We know that God wasn't punishing Job for sinning (see chapters 1 & 2). When bad stuff happens to us, it doesn't mean God is punishing us for a specific sin.

So how is it that we all have problems? Well, it *is* because of *sin*. Right at the beginning, Adam and Eve disobeyed God, and brought sin into the world. Sin has messed up our world, and we all suffer sometimes because of it. The ray of hope is that God often uses bad times to strengthen us and to make us rely on Him. And one day, all Christians will be gathered to the perfect place where there's no more sin or suffering.

SHARE IT

▶ *If someone asked you why there's suffering in the world, how would you answer them?*

PRAY ABOUT IT

When life is tough, don't blame God. And don't wallow, thinking it's because you're so sinful. Turn to God with your problems and ask Him to help you out.

➡ TAKE IT FURTHER

More words from Eliphaz on p113.

23 | Failing friends

Now it's Job's turn to speak. Chapters 1 & 2 made it clear that Job wasn't being punished by God for any sin he'd committed. Job protested his innocence. Sometimes to his friends (chapter 6) and sometimes to God (chapter 7).

👁 Read Job 6 v 1–13

ENGAGE YOUR BRAIN

▶ Which words would you use to describe Job's feelings in each of these sections?
v2–4:
v8–10:
v11–13:

👁 Read verses 14–30

▶ How does Job think his friends should act? (v14)

▶ But how does he describe them? (v15, 26)

▶ Why does he think they're like this? (v21)

▶ What does he ask his friends to prove? (v28–30)

Job is certain he hasn't sinned and that God isn't punishing him for wrongdoing. He doesn't need his friends to turn against him and preach at him during such miserable

times. He needs their support, devotion and comfort (v14).

When people are suffering, they probably don't need us to preach at them. Or to say "I told you so!" They need our support, friendship, prayers and comfort. That often means shutting up and listening to them.

GET ON WITH IT

▶ Who do you need to apologise to for being too preachy?
▶ Who do you need to be more supportive to?
▶ How can you show them God's love and comfort them?

PRAY ABOUT IT

Ask God to help you be a devoted, supportive friend.

THE BOTTOM LINE

Shut up and be supportive.

→ TAKE IT FURTHER

Job talks to God — page 114.

24 Bildad blabbers

Job couldn't understand why God was letting him suffer so much. Eliphaz wrongly told Job it was his own fault. But would Bildad offer more helpful advice?

👁 Read Job 8 v 1–10

ENGAGE YOUR BRAIN

▷ What did Bildad think of Job's complaining? (v2)

▷ Why did He think Job's kids died? (v4)

▷ What did he say was Job's way out of misery? (v5–7)

▷ What else did he suggest? (v8–10)

Oh dear. Bildad is talking rubbish too. Job's kids didn't die because they'd committed terrible sins. God wasn't punishing them.

And it's not true that if Job lived a good life God would make everything perfect for him. The Bible tells us that believers *will* suffer sometimes (1 Peter 1 v 6–7). Our lives won't be perfect until eternal life with Jesus.

👁 Read verses 11–22

▷ What was Bildad's point? (v13)

▷ What pictures does he use to illustrate his point?
v11–13:
v14–15:
v16–22:

People who forget God often seem to do well, living their own way. But one day God will punish those who reject Him. Bildad was right about that. And He was right that God won't reject people who live for Him (v20). But Bildad was dead wrong to assume that Job was an evil man just because God seemed to have left him. God was still with Job.

PRAY ABOUT IT

Thank God that He NEVER leaves those who trust Him. Ask Him to give you the courage and strength to trust Him when life is good and when life is tough.

→ TAKE IT FURTHER

Show me the money! Page 114.

25 | God's great!

**After Bildad's blabber, it's time for Job to reply.
And he's got some big things to say about God.**

👁 Read Job 9 v 1–10

ENGAGE YOUR BRAIN

▶ *How would you sum up Job's description of God? (v5–10)*

▶ *How do humans compare to God? (v2–4)*

👁 Skim read verses 11–35

Job had lost almost everything. But he knew that God had every right to do all this and much more to him.

Job's got most things right so far, though not everything.

What Job got right
- All good things come from God, so God can take them away.
- God can do what He wants.
- Job is nothing compared with God, so he can't argue with God.

What Job got wrong
- God doesn't want to hear Job.
- God would hurt Job for no reason.

Job was wrong about these last two, and he still didn't understand why bad stuff was happening to him. Sometimes we just don't know exactly why bad things happen to good people. But the life and death of Jesus teaches us we can always trust God to do what's best for us.

PRAY ABOUT IT

Read Romans 8 v 28 and use it to praise God. And then use Job 9 v 5–10 to start you off praising God for His power and creation.

→ TAKE IT FURTHER

Job continues on page 114.

26 Zophar so bad

Job's friends aren't being very supportive! Next up is Zophar. Will he be any different or will he give Job a hard time too?

👁 Read Job 11 v 1–6

ENGAGE YOUR BRAIN

▷ *What's Zophar's opinion of what Job's been saying? (v2–3)*
▷ *What does he want God to do? (v5–6)*

Zophar is even less subtle than Eliphaz and Bildad! He thinks Job is stupid to claim to be innocent. Zophar wants God to put Job in his place. And to show Job what true wisdom is (later in the book, God does exactly that — Job 28 v 28).

👁 Read verses 7–12

▷ *What's the answer to the questions in v7?*

Zophar thinks Job is dumb to try and understand why God let him suffer so much. Zophar seems to think God is unknowable. It's true that there are many things our tiny brains can't understand about God. And we won't always understand why He lets certain things happen. But we

can know God. We can have a close relationship with Him. For us, that's made possible by Jesus.

👁 Read verses 13–20

Job's friends think the solution is simple: if only Job would turn from his wicked ways and devote himself to God, then God would reward him with a bright future. But Job wasn't being punished for sinning. So Zophar had got it wrong too.

THINK IT OVER

▷ *Do you try to understand more about God?*
▷ *Do you want to be closer to Him?*
▷ *Do you live to please Him?*

PRAY ABOUT IT

Talk these issues over with God. Say sorry for your failings. Ask Him to help you seek Him more in the Bible; grow closer to Him Jesus; and to give your life to serving Him.

→ TAKE IT FURTHER

No *Take it further* today.

27 Job fights back

Zophar was the latest of Job's "friends" to give him a hard time. As usual, Job replies to the accusations and then talks to God. Job's got loads to say this time, so get ready to speed read!

👁 Speed read Job 12 v 1–12

ENGAGE YOUR BRAIN
- ▷ How does Job sum up his situation? (v4)
- ▷ What great truth does Job reveal about creation? (v10)

👁 Skim verses 13–25
- ▷ What does Job tell us about God?
  v13:
  v14–16:
  v23:

👁 Speed read Job 13 v 1–12
- ▷ What does Job think of his friends' "wisdom"? (v4–5, 12)
- ▷ What does Job want to do? (v3)

👁 Read verses 13–19
- ▷ What's surprising about Job's attitude towards God? (v15–16)

Job's fed up with trying to convince his friends that he's innocent. They just won't listen. So he decides to argue his case with God. Job knows this may lead to his destruction, but he also knows he can trust God to do what's right and fair (v15). It may even lead to him being rescued from his suffering and misery (v16). Later in the book we'll see what happens when Job pleads his case to God.

Christopher Ash puts it like this: *"Even in the depths of his suffering, Job doesn't give up. He loves God, so he says: 'I want to meet God. I want to be right with God. I want to be justified, vindicated, put right with God. Though He may slay me, I will live in hope.' Job sets his hope in God for there's nowhere else he can turn."*

PRAY ABOUT IT
Thank God that whatever happens in life we can trust in His goodness. Thank Him for showing this ultimately by sending His Son to die in our place and rise again to rescue us from sin, suffering and death.

→ TAKE IT FURTHER
Job turns to God with his troubles on page 114.

28 — Who do you think you are?

Earlier, Eliphaz seemed almost gentle and sympathetic as he spoke to Job. Now he changes tone — letting his frustration out and ridiculing Job. Who needs enemies when you've got friends like these?!

👁 Read Job 15 v 1–13

ENGAGE YOUR BRAIN

▶ What does Eliphaz accuse Job of? (v4–6)

▶ Who does he think Job should listen to? (v8, 9–10)

"Who do you think you are, Job, to get angry with us? We were only speaking the truth and trying to console you. God is speaking through us to you so you're really raging against God!"

But their words were not comforting or even true. And definitely not from God. They'd falsely accused Job of sinning — no wonder his eyes flashed with anger (12)!

GET ON WITH IT

▶ Do you ever hurt people by "just being honest" or "trying to help"?

▶ Who do you need to be more sympathetic to?

▶ How will you do it?

👁 Quickly read verses 14–35

Eliphaz claims that wicked people suffer throughout their lives. They are tormented by fear and guilt. As usual, there's a grain of truth in Eliphaz's words. But only a grain. Some people do suffer because of their sin. But many people do wrong all their lives and hardly suffer or feel guilty at all. And many godly people suffer loads. But we can trust that God is faithful and always does what is right.

PRAY ABOUT IT

Ask God to help you to be more sympathetic and understanding in the way you deal with people. Pray for friends who don't seem to care about the sin in their lives. Ask God to show them their need for Jesus' forgiveness.

→ TAKE IT FURTHER

Why do sinful people seem to have a good life? Page 115.

29 Who's on my side?

How do you react when life seems unfair? Do you lash out at those around you? Do you question God? Do you humbly turn to Him in prayer? Do you trust that God's in control? Well, Job did all those things...

👁 Read Job 16 v 1–14

ENGAGE YOUR BRAIN

▷ *What's Job's complaint against his friends? (v2–3)*

▷ *How would he have acted differently in their shoes? (v5)*

▷ *Who does Job know is behind his suffering? (v7, 9, 11)*

Job describes God as a wild animal attacking him. Yet again he questions why so many bad things have happened to a servant of God like him. Has Job finally flipped and turned against God?

👁 Read verses 15–21

▷ *How does Job respond to his suffering? (v15–16)*

▷ *Has he turned against God? (v17)*

▷ *Why does he still cry out to God for help? (v18–21)*

Amazingly, Job doesn't turn against God. Yes, he sulks and complains and feels sorry for himself. Of course he does — he's lost his children, his wealth and he's in constant pain. But Job never reacts in violence and he still turns to God in prayer.

Job knows that his friends won't be able to persuade God to end his suffering. His only hope is that he has a friend in heaven who will plead with God on his behalf. That friend is Jesus. If we turn to Him for forgiveness, He will plead with God for us — and our sins will be washed away. Jesus is on our side. Only He can put us right with God.

PRAY ABOUT IT

Talk to God about this and anything else that's on your mind.

THE BOTTOM LINE

Jesus is our friend and defender.

→ TAKE IT FURTHER

Yep, there's even more on page 115.

30 | A glimmer of hope

At first it seems as if today's chapters are the same old pattern — one of Job's friends (Bildad) giving him a hard time; then Job defending himself and complaining about his suffering. But there's a glimmer of hope for Job!

👁 Read Job 18 v 1–21

ENGAGE YOUR BRAIN

▷ *What's Bildad's jibe at Job this time? (v1–4)*

▷ *What's Bildad's view of what happens to wicked people?*

Bildad claims that all sinful people will be punished in their lifetime. But life doesn't always turn out like that. Sin has made our world unfair. Sinners might not suffer in this life. But they *will* be punished when Jesus returns as Judge.

👁 Skim read Job 19 v 1–22

▷ *How does Job answer Bildad? (v1–6)*

▷ *Choose 3 words that describe Job's view of his life:*

👁 Carefully read verses 23–29

▷ *What's the irony of v23–24?*
▷ *What's incredible about Job's*

words in v25–27?

Job seems to be sinking to new depths of despair (v1–22) only to rise to new heights of faith and hope! This is a real turning point for Job. He's been searching for reasons for his suffering. He's not found any but he comes to a remarkable conclusion: I can trust God; He will vindicate me when I see Him face to face.

Unlike Job, we live after Jesus' death and resurrection. Our Redeemer does live — Jesus Christ, who has bought us back from sin and snatched us from the clutches of death!

PRAY ABOUT IT
I hope you're praising and thanking God already...

THE BOTTOM LINE
I know that my Redeemer lives.

TAKE IT FURTHER
Hope springs eternal on page 115.

31 So unfair!

"Life's not fair!" Have you ever felt like screaming that at the top of your lungs? Job had. In fact, he seems to have been doing it a lot. But his friend Zophar disagreed strongly.

👁 Read Job 20 v 4–11

According to Zophar, what goes around, comes around. If you reject God in this life, then you'll be punished in this life.

ENGAGE YOUR BRAIN

▶ *Do you agree with that?*

▶ *What evidence do you see in the world that supports or disproves Zophar's theory?*

👁 Read Job 21 v 7–16

▶ *What does Job say about the lives of wicked people? (v13)*

▶ *What's their attitude to God? (v14–15)*

▶ *What don't they realise? (v16)*

👁 Read verses 22–26

▶ *What truth about this life does Job point out? (v23–26)*

▶ *What does he say to people who say that God is unfair? (v22)*

The fact is: we live in an unfair world. It's been messed up by sin. Most people don't live God's way. So, of course life is unfair. Some "bad" people seem to have an easy life, and some "good" people seem to have misery piled on them. We often won't understand why.

But can we tell God He's wrong? Definitely not. He is the perfect Judge, who always does the right thing. It may baffle us sometimes, but we can be sure it's for the right reasons. And we can be sure that, at the end of this imperfect life, the wicked will be punished and God's people will go on to a new, perfect life with Him.

PRAY ABOUT IT

Talk to God about anything that's troubling you. Ask Him to help you respond in the right way when the wicked seem to be successful.

→ TAKE IT FURTHER

No *Take it further* today.

Relationships

How far can we go if sex is off limits?
Is it OK to date a non-Christian?
Am I weird if I don't have a boyfriend/girlfriend?

God is clear that sex is an amazing gift and He created it for a man and woman within marriage (see Issues 9 & 14 of Engage). But let's be honest, marriage seems a long way off for most of us! Frustratingly, the Bible doesn't say anything about dating / going out with people — it just didn't exist in Bible times: you were single, engaged or married.

But while the Bible doesn't give us rules about how far we can go between holding hands and jumping into bed with someone, there are clear principles to guide us. As always in the Bible, what's in our hearts is the key, not keeping a set of rules. Thankfully we're not alone — God's Holy Spirit is there to help us!

A MESSY WORLD
Check out 1 Thessalonians 4 v 1–7. The world these Christians lived in was just as messy as ours —

prostitution, adultery, homosexuality, divorce, sleeping around and polygamy. So what can we learn from what Paul wrote to them?

Well, God's aim for us is to be sanctified (v3); to be made holy, more like Jesus. So in our relationships, is our behaviour pleasing God because we are being more like Jesus? And it's also pretty clear what we should avoid — sexual immorality (v3); that means any sexual activity outside marriage. Even when we feel that "everyone else is doing it", we must learn to control our bodies in a way that is holy and honourable (v4). So, learn to control your desires; rather than them controlling you.

TRUE LOVE
So how should we treat other Christians (including our boyfriend or girlfriend)? Don't wrong them or take advantage (v6). So don't

use people just for your own selfish desires. Whether that's spinning out a relationship that's going nowhere or using someone else's body for your own pleasure — even by mutual agreement! Think about Jesus' command to love your neighbour as yourself.

Although marriage might seem a million miles away now, it's God's ultimate design for boy/girl relationships. If they have a choice, Christians should only marry Christians (1 Corinthians 7 v 39). More generally in 2 Corinthians 6 v14, Paul talks about not being *"yoked together with unbelievers"*, saying: *"What fellowship can light have with darkness?"* Why would you want to share your life and your bed with someone who does not share your faith and eternal destination?

This has major implications for when you start dating seriously. If you're dating a non-Christian who you know you could/would never marry, why are you together?

HEALTH WARNING 1
We all screw up and make mistakes, often over and over again, even if we don't want to. We might have done things we deeply regret, or others may have hurt us. God wants us to live His way, which is best for us and brings Him glory — but He loves us and always offers us total forgiveness if we truly repent.

"If we claim to be without sin, we deceive ourselves and the truth is not in us. If we confess our sins, he is faithful and just and will forgive us our sins and purify us from all unrighteousness" (1 John 1 v 8–9).

HEALTH WARNING 2
You are not a second-class citizen if you're not in a relationship! The Bible says marriage and singleness each have advantages and disadvantages but neither is necessarily better than the other. So don't think that your goal in life must be to get a boyfriend/girlfriend. Being single may suck on Valentine's Day, but there are lots of advantages too. Jesus was single all His life, and He was totally fulfilled. The world tries to make out that sex and relationships bring complete personal fulfilment — they don't. Marriage won't exist in the new creation — our relationship with Jesus will.

Galatians

Freedom fighters

Let's set the scene. It's the middle of the 1st century AD. The location is Galatia (now called Turkey). The apostle Paul had been sent far and wide by God to tell people about Jesus and the rescue achieved by His death and resurrection. One of the places Paul visited was Galatia. Some of the people there became Christians and set up their own churches. Brilliant.

But the honeymoon period didn't last long. Infiltrators got into the church and corrupted it with false teaching. They told these new Christians they should obey Jewish law — especially the bit about circumcision for the men. Ouch. Sadly, the Galatian Christians fell for this big lie.

The infiltrators (probably Jewish Christians) seemed to be afraid of what Jews would think and so they watered down the gospel message to make it seem more "acceptable". Instead of teaching that trusting in Jesus is the only way to get right with God, they were saying you need Jesus **plus** other stuff — such as keeping Jewish laws.

Guess what. Paul wasn't happy with this. Not one bit. These false teachers were pulling the Galatian Christians away from the gospel and away from serving God. So Paul wrote them a strongly-worded letter that has challenged and encouraged Christians for centuries.

In Galatians, Paul shows us what true freedom is. Freedom given by Jesus Christ. Freedom from our past, from our guilt before God, from His punishment. Freedom from sin's power. Freedom from religion. And it's a freedom to serve Him willingly, obediently, faithfully. It's a freedom worth fighting for and Paul gives us the weapons we need for the battle.

Paul points out what threatens to drag us back into slavery. Christians have been set free. So stay free.

32 Listen up

If you have something difficult to say to a friend, do you rush in boldly or do you start gently and subtly? Well, Paul doesn't really do subtle, and he wants the Galatians to listen to him.

⊙ Read Galatians 1 v 1–5

ENGAGE YOUR BRAIN

▷ Why should these guys listen to Paul? (v1)

▷ Why should we listen to him?

PRAY ABOUT IT
Thank God for sending Paul and his vital message. Ask the Lord to speak to you through Paul's words in Galatians.

⊙ Read verses 3–5 again

▷ What incredible thing did Jesus do for us? (v3–4)

▷ Why?

▷ So what should our response be? (v5)

SHARE IT

▷ How would you explain what the gospel is, using v3–5?

▷ Who do you need to share these truths with?

Jesus willingly gave Himself as a sacrifice. He died to take the punishment we deserve for our sin. So if we trust in Him, He'll rescue us from sin and the evil in the world around us. So that we're ruled by God and not by sin and evil any more. That's grace (v2) — God giving us an amazing gift we don't deserve and putting us at peace with Him.

PRAY ABOUT IT
So what's the only right response to all this?

→ TAKE IT FURTHER
Listen up for more on Paul and the Galatians on page 115.

33 | Jesus plus

There's no time for small talk. Paul knows the Christians in Galatia are in serious trouble. So he dives straight in at the deep end to face the big issue head on.

👁 Read Galatians 1 v 6–10

ENGAGE YOUR BRAIN

▶ *What has stunned Paul? (v6)*

▶ *What's been happening? (v7)*

▶ *How serious was the problem to Paul? (v8–9)*

Paul had taken the gospel (good news) of Jesus to Galatia. He told them that Jesus is all we need to rescue us from sin and put us right with God. They believed the gospel and trusted in Jesus. Awesome.

But these infiltrators had brought a different gospel (v6) and perverted the amazing truth about Jesus. They'd added to it and watered it down. That's why Paul wasn't pulling his punches. He couldn't believe these Christians had so easily believed this wrong teaching and started turning their backs on God.

This new gospel was a massive insult to Jesus — it was saying His death on the cross isn't enough to put us right with God. As if the way we live can earn us eternal life. Total rubbish.

GET ON WITH IT

If anyone tells you that you need Jesus **plus** something else (special abilities, rules, church etc) to be rescued from sin... don't listen to them. It's all about Jesus and not about anything we can do. Make sure they know that. And tell older Christians if you suspect someone of teaching a different gospel message.

PRAY ABOUT IT

Ask God to silence those who distort the gospel. Ask for His strength so that you and your church / youth group will never turn from the gospel of Jesus crucified for us.

TAKE IT FURTHER

More from Acts on page 115.

34 | From persecutor to preacher

Paul took the message of Jesus to the Galatians. They believed it and Jesus transformed their lives. But they've now been fooled by a new gospel message. So why should they listen to Paul and not these new teachers?

👁 **Read Galatians 1 v 11–12**

ENGAGE YOUR BRAIN

ᴅ *How did Paul receive the message he taught?*

If that really happened, Paul must be telling the truth. But how could the Galatians be sure he's not making it up? Better check the evidence.

👁 **Read verses 13–24**

ᴅ *Fill in the evidence:*

Before (v13–14):

Then (v15–16):

Influence from others (v17–19):

What happened (v21–24):

The evidence spoke for itself. Only God could turn a persecuting bully into a preacher. Paul hadn't got his gospel message from Peter or any of the other apostles. And look at the effect His preaching had in Syria and Cilicia (v23–24). Paul's message must have come from God Himself.

THINK IT OVER

ᴅ *So what does all this tell us about Paul's message in Galatians?*

ᴅ *So what should we do with this teaching?*

ᴅ *How can you make sure you listen to God's message in Galatians?*

PRAY ABOUT IT

Ask God to speak to you clearly through Galatians. Pray that you'll put His teaching into practice. Now think of 3 people you can't imagine becoming Christians. Ask God to turn their lives around, as He did with Paul.

➔ **TAKE IT FURTHER**
More of Paul's story on page 116.

35 | It's all about Jesus

Remember the infiltrators? They told Christians that trusting in Jesus wasn't enough. To be right with God, you needed to follow Jewish laws, such as getting circumcised. That would be a painful change for Titus...

👁 Read Galatians 2 v 1–5

Paul and Titus stuck to their guns. Titus trusted in Jesus' death to rescue him and put him right with God. He didn't need to get circumcised or do anything else. Jesus is enough.

👁 Read verses 6–10

ENGAGE YOUR BRAIN

▷ *Why didn't Paul care about people's reputations? (v6)*

▷ *What did Paul and Peter have in common? (v7–8)*

▷ *And what did they all think was important? (v10)*

It doesn't really matter what image we have, or if we're popular or well-respected. God is interested in our hearts — whether or not we love Him and live for Him.

Paul was very different from James, Peter and John. But they all loved God and wanted to tell people about Jesus. So they welcomed Paul and showed him friendship.

You might know Christians who go to a different kind of church from you. They might be a bit different. But if they trust in Jesus, they're in God's family with you! And you shouldn't shun them or criticise them.

GET ON WITH IT

▷ *Which fellow Christians do you need to work harder at getting along with?*

▷ *What will you do?*

▷ *And how can you make sure you remember the poor? (v10)*

PRAY ABOUT IT

Talk to God about anything He's challenged you with today.

TAKE IT FURTHER

Poors for thought on page 116.

36 Paul vs Peter

When Paul went to Jerusalem, Peter welcomed him. When Peter visited Paul in Antioch, guess what happened. Paul welcomed... oh, hold on...

👁 Read Galatians 2 v 11–14

ENGAGE YOUR BRAIN

▶ What was the shock for Peter? (v11)

▶ What was Paul's problem with Peter? (v12–13)

▶ Why was it so important that Paul confronted Peter? (v14)

It seems that Peter and others were scared of a group of Jewish Christians. So they started shunning people from non-Jewish (Gentile) backgrounds. And were forcing them to follow Jewish customs such as circumcision. Paul spoke out because he was worried people would think that trusting in Jesus' death wasn't enough to put you right with God.

👁 Read verses 15–16

Justified = being put right with God; having your sins forgiven by Him. Only trusting in Jesus can justify you. These guys were also relying on obeying laws to justify them. So Paul told them they were wrong — it's all about Jesus, not anything we can do. Peter compromised his beliefs because he was scared of the influential "circumcision group".

THINK IT OVER

▶ Whose opinion might cause you to compromise your beliefs?

▶ What could this lead to?

PRAY ABOUT IT

Praise God for giving you everything you need in Jesus. Pray that you won't let fear of certain people affect your beliefs or how you share your faith with others.

THE BOTTOM LINE

Jesus is all we need.

TAKE IT FURTHER

No Take it further today.

37 | Sin? So what?

"Hey, Paul! If keeping the law doesn't make you right with God, can we sin as much as we like? It sounds as if Jesus is encouraging us to sin!" Brace yourself for Paul's answer.

👁 Read Galatians 2 v 17–18

ENGAGE YOUR BRAIN

▶ How does Paul answer the claim that it's OK to sin?

If we mess up sometimes and sin (as we all do), it's our fault, not Jesus'. Some people have this outlook: "If God has forgiven all your sin, then you can do whatever you want." But the Christian life doesn't work like that. When you become a Christian, your life is changed and you want to start living God's way.

👁 Read verses 19–20

Jesus died in our place. When we trust in what He's done for us, our sins are forgiven. It's as if our old sinful life has died too. As a Christian, you no longer live for yourself, but for Jesus. So Christians no longer want to sin; they want to please Jesus.

👁 Read verse 21

Paul's final blow is devastating. If we try to get right with God by being good, we're saying that Jesus' death was pointless. We're throwing God's grace back in His face. But Jesus' death was essential — it was the defining moment in history. And only by trusting in His sacrifice for us can we be forgiven.

SHARE IT

▶ If someone said: "It doesn't really matter if you sin", how would answer them?

▶ What about if someone claimed that living a good life will **get** them to heaven?

▶ Who can you talk to about getting better at explaining the gospel?

THE BOTTOM LINE

I live by faith in the Son of God, who loved me and gave himself for me.

→ TAKE IT FURTHER

Follow the Roman road to page 116.

38 | You foolish Galatians!

Paul not only gave Peter a hard time, he now had to pile into the Galatians. Frankly, what on earth did they think they were doing?

👁 **Read Galatians 3 v 1–5**

ENGAGE YOUR BRAIN

▶ How would you describe Paul's tone here?

▶ What's the answer to the question in v2?

▶ What about v5?

▶ Yet how were these believers living? (v3)

They stopped trusting Jesus. They tried to make themselves good enough for God. But nothing we can do can put us right with God. Only Jesus can do that. We keep banging on about the only way to get right with God. But that's because it's so important. So we'll keep on telling you until it gets right into your brain and your heart!

👁 **Read verses 6–9**

▶ What's been the right response to God all along? (v6–7)

▶ What's exciting about God's great plan? (v8–9)

The whole Bible is pointing to Jesus — even the book of Genesis. God promised Abraham that all nations would be blessed through him. Centuries later, Jesus was born into Abe's family. The blessing was the best one ever — the chance for anyone to be forgiven because of Jesus' death and resurrection.

Abraham showed faith — he trusted God's promises. And he was considered right with God. It's the same for the Galatians and for us too — if we trust God and have faith in Jesus, we'll be put right with God.

PRAY ABOUT IT

Christians have so much to thank God for. Write a quick *Thanks List* and then use it as you pray.

→ **TAKE IT FURTHER**

Don't be foolish, turn to page 116.

47

39 | Cursed things first

So... the only way to get right with God is to trust in Jesus' death for us. Yet loads of people still think that living a good life is enough. You probably know a few.

👁 Read Galatians 3 v 10–12

ENGAGE YOUR BRAIN

So we have 2 choices of how to live

Faith in JESUS

Faith in ourselves

Trusting in Jesus to rescue us by dying for us

Trusting in our own efforts to please God

If we could keep all of God's laws and never disobey Him, that would be enough. But we all disobey God at some time. Whether it's lies, jealousy or not honouring our parents. We all mess up and deserve God's punishment. We're all cursed.

👁 Read verses 13–14

▶ *What shocking step has Jesus taken? (v13)*

▶ *So what's true for people who trust the gospel?*

Because of our sin, we're all cursed to be punished by God. But our curse was transferred to Jesus when He took that punishment, on our behalf, on the cross. And that's not all. Jesus also gives us His Holy Spirit (v14) to live in us and help us live for God.

PRAY ABOUT IT

There must be loads you want to say to God today.

THE BOTTOM LINE

Jesus takes God's punishment on our behalf. And He gives us His Spirit.

➔ TAKE IT FURTHER

There's a little bit more to be found on page 116.

40 ¦ Point of law

Paul's been talking loads about "the law" and God's "promise". The law = God's Old Testament law, given to His people though Moses. God's promise to Abraham was that He'd rescue everyone who trusts God.

👁 Read Galatians 3 v 15–18

ENGAGE YOUR BRAIN
▶ What would you say is Paul's main point here?

How about this? We can inherit amazing things from God, such as forgiveness and eternal life with Him. We can't earn this inheritance by keeping God's law. It's a free gift to everyone who trusts in Jesus.

If we can't get right with God by keeping His law, what's the point of God's law?

👁 Read verses 19–25
We all try to live good lives but we all disobey God. Trying to keep God's laws shows us how often we mess up. It shows us that we do sin and we can't live lives good enough for God.

We can't get right with God by living good lives. So we need someone to rescue us from sin and put us right with God. Only Jesus can do that.

So we need to trust Him to rescue us. God's law isn't pointless. It points us to Christ so that we'll turn to Him.

THINK IT OVER
▶ What should be your attitude to God's law in the Bible?

▶ What should you do when it highlights your sin?

PRAY ABOUT IT
Thank God for giving you His law to show up your sin and point you to Jesus. Spend time confessing your sins and thanking Him for the forgiveness offered by Jesus.

➔ TAKE IT FURTHER
2000 years in 7 verses — page 117.

The Bible timeline

One of the main ambitions of **engage** is to encourage you to dive into God's word, learning how to handle it and understand it more. Each issue, TOOLBOX gives you tips, tools and advice for wrestling with the Bible. This issue, we look at the timeline of the Bible.

Have you broken any of God's commandments this week? And have you slaughtered any female goats as a sin offering? No? Why not? That's what the Bible says people should do in Leviticus 4 v 27–31! So how do we know which commands apply directly to us and which don't? We need to know our Bible timeline.

ONE BIG STORY

The Bible is a book with a big story that slowly unfolds throughout human history. It begins at the start of Genesis with God creating the heavens and the earth (Genesis 1 v 1). It ends in the final chapters of Revelation with God's people living with Him in a perfect new world, with God's enemies punished in hell.

Loads happens in between! The most important events are probably the Fall (where sin entered and ruined God's perfect world) and the death and resurrection of Jesus (where things were put right). We can arrange those events in a simple Bible timeline:

CREATION OF THE WORLD

DEATH AND RESURRECTION OF JESUS

JESUS RETURNS TO JUDGE HEAVEN AND HELL

THE FALL

When you read the Bible, ask three simple questions:

1. Where is this passage on the Bible timeline?
2. Where am I on the Bible timeline?
3. How do I read this passage in the light of things that have happened in between?

Between the time of the Leviticus goat sacrifice passage and now, Jesus' death and resurrection has happened. His death was the final sacrifice for sins. For this reason, we don't have to sacrifice goats any more.

That doesn't mean Leviticus has nothing to say to us. It teaches us that sin is very serious, that a death is needed to deal with it, that only by the shedding of blood can there be forgiveness. We just have to read it through the lens of Christ's death to understand that those sacrifices have now been fulfilled.

DO IT YOURSELF

Read Genesis 13 v 14–17

Some Christians take this to mean we should help modern-day Israel to evict the Palestinians from the Gaza Strip, since God has given the Israelites that land. What do you think of that idea? Try using the three key questions.

1. Where is this passage on the Bible timeline?
2. Where am I on the Bible timeline?
3. How do I read this in the light

of things that have happened in between? In particular, read Hebrews 11 v 16 to see what we're told about the "promised land".

What is the true promised land that Christians are looking forward to?

THE EXCEPTION

We don't need to employ the Bible timeline when looking at God's character. God is unchanging. In every single book of the Bible we read about the very same holy, consistent, perfect God.

"I the Lord do not change"
(Malachi 3 v 6).

"Jesus Christ is the same yesterday and today and for ever"
(Hebrews 13 v 8).

But if you're unsure how a Bible passage applies to you in the 21st century, get out your Bible timeline and ask yourself those 3 questions.

Ideas taken from Dig Deeper by Nigel Beynon and Andrew Sach. Published by IVP and available from The Good Book Company website. Also check out the excellent book God's Big Picture, by Vaughan Roberts.

Proverbs

Wise up!

See that guy over there? Yeah, the one with his head in his cereal bowl. So lazy he can't even be bothered to lift the spoon to his mouth. Some days he doesn't even get out of bed. That's Mr Slob. Some call him Sluggard.

And that one over there — just listen to him talk. Well, he'll talk at you whether you like it or not. He's Motormouth and he just loves the sound of his own voice. And be careful not to share anything confidential with him. Unless you want it broadcast to the whole world.

And there's Ms Sleeparound. She's moving in on someone new and he doesn't stand a chance at resisting her scheming seduction.

We all meet people like Mr Slob, Motormouth and Ms Sleeparound in our daily lives. And we need to know how to treat them. And how to avoid becoming like them.

The world Proverbs speaks about is our everyday world. This book has got its feet firmly on the ground, but it's aiming high. Proverbs wants to make us wise. True wisdom, says Proverbs, involves living life for God — as He wants us to live.

So wise up and take Proverbs seriously. Through its pages of advice, wise words and warnings, God will show us how to be wise guys — people who live for Him in a sinful world.

41 | Why bother with Proverbs?

So what's the point of all these proverbs?
And what does it mean to be wise anyway?

👁 **Read Proverbs 1 v 1–6**

ENGAGE YOUR BRAIN

▷ *What are the purposes of Proverbs?*

-
-
-
-
-
-
-

▷ *How would you summarise that in one sentence?*

Proverbs is very user friendly. It's been written specifically so we'll learn loads from it. It's a very practical book, so expect to have your views, thoughts and actions challenged. Get ready to do what it says.

If you want to know what God expects from wise guys, then listen up. If you need discipline or believe in justice, then this is the book for you.

If you're young, old, simple or wise, Proverbs was written for you.

👁 **Read verse 7**

▷ *What's the starting point for knowledge and wisdom?*

Fearing the Lord means taking God seriously. Giving Him the respect He deserves. Living to please Him. Wisdom isn't getting good grades, making clever decisions or having street smarts. What God reveals in His word is the only real basis for understanding what life is all about. So true wisdom is living God's way.

PRAY ABOUT IT

Ask God to help you take Him more seriously. And pray that He will use Proverbs to get you more God-wise.

THE BOTTOM LINE

The fear of the Lord is the beginning of knowledge.

→ **TAKE IT FURTHER**

If you can be bothered, go to p117.

42 | Mum's the word

Be honest, what do you think of advice from parents? Do you usually listen to it or ignore it? What about when you're told who you should or shouldn't hang out with?

👁 Read Proverbs 1 v 8–9

ENGAGE YOUR BRAIN

▶ What does God say to you (through Solomon)? (v8)

▶ What do you think v9 thinks?

You might find this hard to swallow, but our parents do actually know quite a lot. You may think they're out of touch or don't understand you. But get this — God says listen to their advice. Don't ignore them. Honour them and obey them.

GET ON WITH IT

▶ How exactly do you need listen to your parents more?

▶ What advice should you stop ignoring?

👁 Read verses 10–19

▶ What's the advice here? (v10)

▶ What happens to people who try to get rich dishonestly? (v18–19)

GET ON WITH IT

▶ How do you behave when you're around your friends?

▶ Do you go along with the crowd or obey God?

▶ Who encourages you to do stuff you know is wrong?

▶ What should you do about it?

▶ How will you avoid temptation?

THE BOTTOM LINE

Here are two simple but difficult ways to please God. Obey your parents and stand up to friends who encourage you to sin.

PRAY ABOUT IT

Ask God, through His Spirit, to help you live for Him. Tell Him about the things you struggle with. Talk to Him about your parents and your friends.

→ TAKE IT FURTHER

Walk on over to page 117.

43 | The voice of wisdom

Lady Wisdom is standing on her soapbox and she's got plenty to shout about.

👁 Read Proverbs 1 v 20–33

ENGAGE YOUR BRAIN

▷ *Who was she talking to? (v22)*

▷ *What did they fail to do? (v23–25)*

▷ *What's their attitude? (v29)*

These people were stupid. That doesn't mean they failed at school. They were dumb because they didn't take God seriously. They ignored true wisdom and refused to live life the right way — to please God. The stupidest thing anyone can do is ignore God.

▷ *What would happen to them? (v30–32)*

▷ *How will God treat people who have ignored Him? (v28)*

▷ *What about people who listen to God? (v33)*

Taking God seriously means taking Jesus Christ seriously. He's the only way to God. Anyone who ignores or rejects the message of Jesus will discover, one day, that God has rejected them. We're called to listen to God and to accept the truth of Jesus — and one day Jesus will give us eternal safety and security.

PRAY ABOUT IT

Pray that you'll listen to true wisdom in Proverbs. And ask God to help you know Jesus Christ better.

THE BOTTOM LINE

Don't ignore God and His wisdom.

→ TAKE IT FURTHER

More wise words on page 117.

44 | Walk this way

Have you got a swagger or a limp? Do you walk in a distinctive way or just like everyone else? Proverbs says: "Walk this way — God's way, avoiding the obstacles and traps of sin."

👁 Read Proverbs 2 v 1–11

ENGAGE YOUR BRAIN

▶ *What are the 4 steps to getting wisdom? (v1–4)*

1.

2.

3.

4.

▶ *Why is it worth the effort? (v5)*

▶ *What are some of the benefits of being truly wise? (v9–11)*

Yes, there are things we can do to step towards wisdom, but it's not something we achieve for ourselves. It's God who gives us wisdom, knowledge and understanding (v6). He protects those who are wise — who respect Him and live His way. Victory will be theirs! (v7)

👁 Read verses 12–22

▶ *What will being wise and living for God protect us from?*
v12–15:
v16:

Being wise means walking God's way (v20). It's the path to the promised land (v21) — perfect, eternal life with God. But not everyone will follow the path to God's land (v22).

GET ON WITH IT

Look at verses 12–19 again.

▶ *Is there anyone you need to be wise about, and stop spending time with?*

▶ *What can you do to make sure you avoid sexual sin?*

PRAY ABOUT IT

Talk to God about these things. Ask Him to help you live wisely. Thank Him for the promise of eternal life.

→ TAKE IT FURTHER

No *Take it further* today.

45 Live long and prosper

Do you want a long and prosperous life? Want to make a name for yourself? Want a life of love and faithfulness? Want to be healthy? Then listen up.

Read Proverbs 3 v 1–8

ENGAGE YOUR BRAIN

▶ *Write down the commands and the benefits found in these verses:*

COMMAND	BENEFIT
v1	v2
v3	v4
v5-6	v6
v7	v8

Solomon isn't saying that all believers will be rich and super healthy! The Hebrew word here for prosperity is "shalom" — peace, happiness and fullness of life. Obeying God's commands will be really tough sometimes but it leads to a fuller life, which will one day be perfect in eternity.

God expects our constant love and faithfulness (v3). Being wise doesn't mean relying on our own knowledge — it involves trusting God completely and relying on Him (v5). Giving Him the glory as He guides you through life (v6). Walking His way and running from sin.

PRAY ABOUT IT

Admit to God the times you've not trusted that He knows what's best for you. Pray that you'll believe that His ways will always be what's best.

→ TAKE IT FURTHER

Follow the path to page 117.

46 : What wisdom's worth

More wise words from Solomon. These proverbs involve barns, silver, gold, rubies, trees, clouds, necklaces and snares. But mostly they're about seeking wisdom and serving God.

👁 Read Proverbs 3 v 9–12

Give God the best of what you've got — money, possessions, abilities. After all, He's the one who gave you those things. And don't resent it when God challenges you and teaches you hard lessons. God disciplines you because He loves you so much and longs for you to live His way.

👁 Read Proverbs 3 v 13–16

ENGAGE YOUR BRAIN

▶ *How do v16–18 show us what eternal life will be like?*

▶ *How does God's world point us to His wisdom? (v19–20)*

▶ *Why is wisdom worth holding on to? (v21–26)*

True wisdom — honouring God with the way we live — is precious and essential. It's so easy to rely on our own abilities, especially when life is hard. But it's pointless: we should put our confidence and trust in the Lord.

How do we know we can trust God? Just look at the world around you. God created our wonderful world — that's how wise and powerful He is. We can trust Him to help us through life in the world He created.

Being wise means trusting in Jesus to rescue us from sin. That's the only way to real, eternal, peaceful life with God. True wealth, health and happiness can only be found in eternity with Jesus.

GET ON WITH IT

Think back to v9–12.

▶ *How can you honour God this week with what He's given you?*

▶ *What discipline/teaching from God do you need to accept?*

▶ *What do you need to do about it?*

Talk these things over with the Lord.

→ TAKE IT FURTHER

Be disciplined and go to page 117.

47 | Wise advice

Being wise isn't about boosting your brain power. It's much more practical than that. Here's some advice on how to be wise in everyday life.

👁 **Read Proverbs 3 v 27–28**

ENGAGE YOUR BRAIN

▶ *How have you done this recently?*

▶ *What positive action will you take?*

👁 **Read verses 29–30**

▶ *Any schemes or false accusations recently?*

▶ *Who do you treat more harshly than you should?*

▶ *What positive action will you take?*

👁 **Read verses 31–35**

▶ *Who do you look up to who isn't a godly role model?*

If we need any reasons for following all this advice, they come in verses 32–35. God hates it when people sin. He will mock, punish and shame anyone who rejects Him.

But those who serve Him are blessed in brilliant ways. They'll be honoured, given grace and their homes are blessed too. Best of all, they're taken into God's confidence. He trusts them and has a personal relationship with them. We can be close to God, the creator of the universe! Incredible.

PRAY ABOUT IT

Think back to the earlier questions and talk to God about how you can live more wisely. You can only do it with His help.

➡ **TAKE IT FURTHER**

More about being taken into God's confidence on page 118.

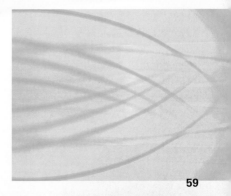

Life and death of a missionary

Jim Elliot wanted to be a missionary from a young age. He became a Christian when he was six and spoke out for Jesus at school. At college, Jim's grades were not that great, and in a letter to his parents, he explained that studying the Bible was much more important to him.

LATIN AMERICAN ADVENTURES

While at college, Jim became more and more interested in missionary work — wanting to spread the message of Jesus around the world. Jim and his friend, Ron Harris, spent a summer in Mexico, working with and learning from a missionary family.

After graduating from college in 1952, Jim went to Ecuador to work among the Quechua people with Peter Fleming. For more than three years they lived among the people, establishing a missionary post in an abandoned oil station. It was close to the little-known Auca tribe and had its own airstrip. In October 1953, Jim married college friend Elisabeth Howard. Their daughter, Valerie, was born two years later. Jim and Elisabeth worked together in translating the New Testament into the Quechua language at the new mission station.

VICIOUS TRIBE

The Aucas were a violent and murderous tribe who'd never had any contact with the outside world. Jim wanted to take the gospel to them, despite the risks. Besides him and his wife, Jim's team consisted of five more missionary couples.

The men discovered the huts of the Auca tribe with the help of missionary jungle pilot, Nate Saint. The first attempt to contact them was by plane. They would fly around the camp shouting friendship words in the Auca language through a loud speaker and dropping down gifts in a basket. Encouraged by this progress, after three months of gift dropping, they decided to make a base on the

Curaray River. They eventually made contact with the Aucas, and after a little persuasion, they were able to convince them to be allowed into their village. Encouraged by this visit, the men felt it was time to go in and try to share the gospel with them.

A SUDDEN END

One morning, the men radioed their wives, saying that they were going to go into the village and would radio them again later. But before this could happen, a group of around twenty Aucas went to the base. "Guys, the Aucas are coming!" As soon as the others heard this, they flew into action, straightening up their camp. Little did these five men know that this would be their last few hours of life. Jim Elliot's body was found down stream with four others. Their bodies had been brutally pierced with spears and hacked by machetes.

A NEW BEGINNING

To many people it seemed that Jim Elliot's dream and the aspirations of the other men had ended in failure. But they had done what was expected of them and it was now time for God to continue with His plan. Among the men's personal possessions was a camera containing photos of the Aucas who had initially made contact with the missionaries. The people in the photographs were recognised by an exiled Auca woman who had helped the missionaries learn the language. They were relatives she thought were dead!

She made contact with them and, before long, Elisabeth Elliot and Rachel Saint (Nate's sister) were actually living with the tribe. They established a church and many of the Aucas became Christians. Elisabeth returned home to America after several years but Rachel stayed with the Aucas for many years.

The love of Christ shown through their forgiveness allowed them to have amazing success with this once murderous tribe. Jim's life was not a waste. In fact, God used his death to bring life through salvation to many Aucas and encouragement and inspiration to thousands of believers worldwide. The deaths of these men, a personal tragedy for their families, have become a testimony of faith in Christ and dedication to the work of God.

48 Job: Why me?

The story so far: Satan claimed Job only served God because he had an easy life. Yet with his family, wealth and health taken from him, Job still didn't turn against God. But he didn't understand why he was suffering. And his friends still claimed it was because he'd sinned loads.

👁 Read Job 22 v 1–11

ENGAGE YOUR BRAIN

▶ What point was Eliphaz making? (v2–3)

▶ What did he accuse Job of? (v4–9)

Eliphaz started out by gently trying to persuade Job to turn back to God (chapter 4). But now he was resorting to vicious lies. Job lived for God. None of these accusations were true. When reasoning fails, people often resort to spreading nasty rumours and lies about Christians.

👁 Read verses 12–20

Eliphaz was saying: "God is above everything, so how can humans stand up to Him? Job, you're just like the sinners who think God can't harm them. But now God's punishing them." Yep, Eliphaz is talking garbage again.

👁 Read verses 21–30

▶ What steps should someone take if they want to turn back to God?
v21:
v22:
v27:

▶ What does Eliphaz claim will happen? (v23, 25, 28)

Eliphaz is right that sinners need to turn back to God and obey Him. But he's wrong to say that people who turn to God will be rewarded with wealth and have all their wishes granted. And he's also wrong to assume that Job needs to turn back to God. Job may be gloomy, but he's never turned his back on God.

PRAY ABOUT IT

Ask God, by His Holy Spirit, to help you stand firm against opposition. Even when people spread lies about you. Ask God to help you continue to honour Him with your life.

→ TAKE IT FURTHER

What would Jesus do? Page 118.

49 Distant deity?

"If only I could talk to God face to face."
"God seems so far away."
"God is terrifying and has a cruel side."
Can you identify with any of those thoughts?

Read Job 23 v 1–7

ENGAGE YOUR BRAIN

▶ What's Job complaining about? (v2–3)

▶ What does he want to do? (v4–5)

Job can't understand why he's suffering so much even though he's always lived for God. He just wants the chance to explain things to God, so the Lord might end Job's suffering. Do you ever feel like that? If only you could explain things to God, He might make everything better.

Read verses verses 8–17

▶ What's the problem? (v8–9)

▶ What else is getting Job down? (v13–14)

▶ How does this make Job feel? (v15–17)

▶ Yet what hope does he hold on to? (v10)

Wherever Job looks, God doesn't seem to be there. God seems so distant. And so terrifying.

THINK IT OVER

Can you understand how Job feels? God seems so far away from you? It seems impossible to talk to Him? Most people feel like that sometimes. But God doesn't leave His people! God always knows what His people are doing. He's always with them, even when it doesn't feel like it.

PRAY ABOUT IT

Because of Jesus, you can go to God and tell Him exactly how you feel. Just pour it out to God; He's listening. He knows all about you, and cares for you. Talk to Him right now.

THE BOTTOM LINE

God's not far away — He's with you and wants to listen to you.

➔ TAKE IT FURTHER

It's not fair! Go to page 118.

50 | God's greatness

Eliphaz, Bildad and Zophar have been harassing Job for ages — telling him how sinful he is. But they've run out of steam. One final blast from Bildad is met by sarcasm from Job.

👁 Read Job 25 v 1–6

ENGAGE YOUR BRAIN

▷ How would you sum up Bildad's opinion of God? (v2–3)

▷ And what about humans? (v6)

We're all pathetic compared to God. None of us can stand before God and claim innocence. The great news for Christians is that Jesus stands before God in our place. Because of Jesus, we can be right with God.

👁 Read Job 26 v 1–14

▷ How would you describe Job's reply to Bildad? (v1–4)

▷ What about Job's description of God? (v5–14)

This is a powerful picture of God. He's so mighty. Nothing is out of His control. No other powers (such as the beasts in v12–13) are a match for God. We can clearly see that God is powerful and wise, yet our understanding barely scratches the surface of how great God is (v14)

👁 Skim read Job 27 v 1–23

▷ Despite his suffering, has Job turned against God? (v2–4)

▷ How does God deal with those who reject Him? (v13–23)

THINK IT OVER

▷ What's your opinion of God? How would you describe Him?

▷ Why should you live God's way rather than your own way?

▷ How are you living right now?

PRAY ABOUT IT

Spend time praising God for His wisdom and power. Thank Him for loving pathetic humans like us. Ask Him to help you devote yourself to Him and not turn away from Him.

→ TAKE IT FURTHER

Why do bad things happen? P 118.

51 | Treasure hunt

Are you ready for a break from all the misery of Job? Well, chapter 28 plunges down into the depths again. But not the depths of depression — we're going down to the very depths of the earth in search of great treasure.

👁 Read Job 28 v 1–19

ENGAGE YOUR BRAIN

▷ *How much trouble do people go to, to find silver, gold and precious stone? (v1–11)*

▷ *What treasure is greater? (v12)*

▷ *But what's the problem? (v13)*

We've already discovered in Proverbs how valuable true, godly wisdom is. Job tells us it's more precious than gold, silver or expensive jewels (v15–19). We should chase after it much more than any earthly possessions.

👁 Read verses 20–28

▷ *Who alone knows how to get truly wise?*

▷ *How does God define wisdom and understanding? (v28)*

We can't expect to find wisdom by ourselves. Wisdom comes from God

— only God can give it to us. Being truly wise means "fearing the Lord". Knowing how weak and sinful we are and how great and holy God is. It means giving God the respect, honour and love He deserves. That's true wisdom!

It also means turning our backs on evil. If we love and respect God, then we'll want to stop doing things that anger Him. We'll want to stop living our way and start living God's way.

PRAY ABOUT IT

Ask God to make you truly wise. Pray that you'll fear Him and live for Him, with the help of the Holy Spirit. Ask Him to help you to shun evil — pray about specific sins you struggle with. And pray all these things for at least three other Christians you know.

→ TAKE IT FURTHER

More wise words on page 119.

52

Job the defendant

Job is in court, trying to prove that he's a good man who serves the Lord. He's about to sum up his case and try to prove his innocence to God.

👁 Skim read Job 29 v 1–25

ENGAGE YOUR BRAIN

▶ What was Job's life like before he lost everything?

▶ What did people think of him?

▶ Who was responsible for it all? (v2–5)

When life is going well for us, God is often forgotten. We should take a leaf out of Job's book and give God the glory when things are going well.

👁 Skim read Job 30 v 1–31

▶ What is Job's life like now?

▶ How do people treat him?

▶ Who does Job say is behind his suffering? (v11, 19–23)

👁 Skim read Job 31 v 1–40

▶ How many different sins does Job list?

▶ How many does he say he's committed?

▶ What does Job want from God?

Job says that he's always obeyed God, so can't understand why he's suffering. But God isn't punishing him for anything. Sometimes people just have a tough time. We can't explain it. We can only ask God to help us.

PRAY ABOUT IT

It's impossible for us to live perfect lives. We'll sometimes mess up. But we can say sorry to God, pick ourselves up and start living His way again. Say sorry to God for some of the bad things you've done this week. Ask Him to help you to start living His way again. And remember to thank Him for the good things in your life.

→ TAKE IT FURTHER

I can't think up any clever reasons, so just go to page 119. Please!

53

Eliphaz, Bildad and Zophar have finally given up trying to persuade Job that he's suffering as punishment for sinning. Quiet at last! Er, no. Young Elihu is next to arrive and he has loads to get off his chest.

👁 **Read Job 32 v 1–5**

ENGAGE YOUR BRAIN

▶ *Why was Elihu angry with Job? (v2)*

▶ *Why was he angry with Job's friends? (v3)*

In verses 6–22, Elihu says he'd kept quiet so far because he was younger than the others. And because he wanted to hear Job's defence. Now he can't keep quiet!

👁 **Read Job 33 v 1–13**

Job couldn't understand why he was suffering. He thought he was innocent, so he asked God for answers. Eliphaz said Job had no right to argue with God, who's so much greater than him.

👁 **Read verses 14–22**

▶ *How did Elihu claim God gets people to turn back to Him?*
v15–18:
v19–22:

God does use many different ways to speak to people and warn them about their sin. In the Bible, we sometimes see God using visions or even illness, pain and disasters to call people back to Him.

Elihu was talking about falling into a dark pit. To die without knowing God is like falling into a disgusting pit that no one can ever get out of. But God gives us loads of warnings! The Bible is packed with warnings that we need to turn away from our sinful lives and start living God's way. He even sent Jesus to rescue us.

PRAY ABOUT IT

Is there anything you want to talk to God about today?

→ **TAKE IT FURTHER**

Elihu continues on page 119.

54 | Big rant

Know anyone who just doesn't stop talking? Well, Elihu is one of those people. He's let himself get worked up and now he's overflowing with anger. Brace yourself as we dip into parts of his long rant against Job.

Read Job 34 v 10–15, 21–30

▷ *What truth about God does Elihu mention in v10–15?*

▷ *Does God act fairly or unfairly? (v21–28)*

Elihu is right that God is always fair. But he's wrong that God always punishes the wicked in this life. God will punish sin on Judgment Day, even though some sinners seem to go unpunished in this life.

Read Job 35 v 9–16

▷ *Why does Elihu think God remains silent? (v10–13)*

▷ *So what does Elihu think of Job? (v14–16)*

Elihu is wrong that God only hears us when our motives are totally pure or when there's no sin in our hearts. If that was always true, no one could ever know God's rescue. We all deserve punishment. Yet God still sent Jesus to rescue sinners like us.

Read Job 37 v 14–24

▷ *What point does Elihu make in v14–19?*

▷ *What's Elihu's summary of his long argument? (v21–24)*

Elihu's long-winded rant is a mixed bag. There are some great truths about God but there's plenty of nonsense too. And, like the other three ranters, he's completely wrong about Job.

Some people give us great advice and teach us about God. Others will mislead us and fill our minds with untruths. And some do a bit of both. We have to test what people say against God's word. If it's in line with the Bible, it's good stuff. If it disagrees with God's word, then it's rubbish.

PRAY ABOUT IT

Talk to God about anything He's challenged you with today.

Tomorrow: God speaks.

55 | God speaks

For the last 35 chapters, Job and his friends have been chatting (well, arguing), trying to work out why God let Job suffer so much. But now a storm is brewing, and God is going to speak.

👁 Read Job 38 v 1–15

ENGAGE YOUR BRAIN

▶ What does God think of Job's anger? (v2)

▶ What are the answers to God's questions?
v4:
v8:
v12–13:

Job had dared to question God's actions, without even beginning to understand God! Job wasn't around when God created the world. Job doesn't even know how big the earth is. So there's no chance he could understand how everything is controlled, and how God does things.

👁 Read verses 16–30

▶ What else does Job not understand?
v17:
v18:
v19:
v22–30:

God is awesome! He can do anything, go anywhere. He controls both light and darkness. The weather is at His command. God understands everything. Of course Job can't do any of the things God can!

👁 Read verses 31–38

Job had to be humbled to realise he is very very small compared with God's greatness! It's easy to complain at God or blame Him when bad things happen. But we need to shut up and listen! We know zilch compared to God, so we need to listen to Him and what He tells us in the Bible.

PRAY ABOUT IT

Thank God that even though He's so big and powerful, He loves tiny you! Ask Him to help you shut up and listen to Him more often.

THE BOTTOM LINE

Shut up and listen to God.

→ TAKE IT FURTHER

Jesus and creation — page 120.

56 Creature comfort

Job wants to know why he's suffering so much. He wants answers from God. So why is God talking about lions, goats and donkeys?

Read Job 38 v 39 – 39 v 12

ENGAGE YOUR BRAIN

▶ Can Job provide food for lions and ravens or understand how animals give birth?

▶ What are the answers to God's other questions?
v5:
v9–10:

Read Job 39 v 13–30

▶ What's God's opinion of the ostrich? (v13–18)

▶ What are the answers to the questions in v19, 20, 26, 27?

God must have a sense of humour — He created the ostrich! He also gave it amazing speed. And He made horses so impressive and fearless. The incredible flight and hunting skills of birds of prey are all down to God.

Through this speech, God is reminding Job how powerful, wise and impressive He is. How can mere humans like Job, and ourselves, think we have the right to argue with God?

We can't possibly hope to understand Him. And yet we sometimes act as if we know better than God. Crazy. God doesn't need to defend Himself or explain why suffering happens. He's the Creator of the universe. We must bow down before Him and accept that His plans are always best.

THINK IT OVER

▶ How has Job helped change your view of God?

▶ How do you need to treat Him differently?

PRAY ABOUT IT

Think of what impresses you in God's creation. Which creatures remind you how great our Creator God is? Spend time praising God for these things.

➔ TAKE IT FURTHER

Fly on over to page 120.

57 | Job silenced

Are you a big talker or a good listener? Job had said plenty about how fed up he was and how God had no reason to make him suffer. Now it's God's turn to question Job.

👁 **Read Job 40 v 1–5**

ENGAGE YOUR BRAIN

▶ What had Job's attitude been towards God? (v2)

▶ How did it change? (v3–5)

Job has no more arguments left. He realises how small and feeble he is compared to God. So he stops himself saying anything else — he knows he's already said too much. That's a big change in Job's attitude.

👁 **Read verses 6–14**

Job, a mere, ordinary, sinful man had dared to doubt God's fairness. It's almost funny that ordinary people like us dare to question the great, holy, perfect, powerful, infinitely wise God!

It's good to ask big questions and wonder why bad things happen. But don't make the mistake of blaming God. We might not understand why bad stuff happens, but we can be confident that God is always fair and His plans are perfect.

👁 **Read verses 15–24**

No one is sure if the behemoth is a hippo or an elephant or a brontosaurus. But we do know that it's one of the most impressive creatures God created (v19) and that only God can tame it! How can weak little humans like us dare to challenge and accuse our all-powerful God? We should bow down and worship Him!

PRAY ABOUT IT

Do that right now as you pray to our astonishing, perfect, all-powerful Creator God.

→ **TAKE IT FURTHER**

Suffering in silence. Page 120.

58

Simply the beast

God is still speaking to Job. It's probably not the response he was expecting, but it's had a huge impact on Job. God finishes off His speech with a long poem about another terrifying beast.

👁 Read Job 41 v 1–34

ENGAGE YOUR BRAIN

▶ *Could Job control this monster?*

▶ *If no one can tame this beast, what does it tell us about God, who can? (v10–11)*

Some people think this terrifying animal is a sea monster or giant crocodile. Others think it symbolises God's enemy, Satan. If humans can't control this beast, how can we expect to stand against God or make claims against Him?

God's response to Job's questions has been surprising. He hasn't explained Job's suffering at all. Instead, He showed Job His great wisdom, so Job couldn't claim God didn't know what He was doing. God showed Job His justice — Job couldn't say God was unfair by letting him suffer. God showed His immense power — Job couldn't claim God wasn't able to carry out His will. God is in control.

👁 Read Job 42 v 1–6

▶ *What has Job realised about...*
God?
himself?
his suffering?

In chapters 1–2, we saw that sin was not the cause of Job's suffering. All along, Job claimed his innocence. He questioned God but never turned away from Him. So why repent? (v6)

Well, Job's just had a staggering personal encounter with God. Job now realises his arrogance at expecting an answer from God — as if God was accountable to him! Job sees that he doesn't know God as well as he should, hence his response.

PRAY ABOUT IT

Thank God that He's in control of everything. Pray that your attitude to Him and to suffering would be right. Pray that you'll know Him better.

→ TAKE IT FURTHER

Why no answers? Try page 120.

59 | Happily ever after

Well done for staying the course. We've reached the end of 42 chapters of suffering, questioning and confusion. Along the way we've learned about ourselves and about our remarkable God. And there's even a happy ending...

👁 **Read Job 42 v 7–9**

ENGAGE YOUR BRAIN
- ▷ Why was God angry with Job's friends?
- ▷ What were they required to do?
- ▷ What does God call Job, 4 times?

It's official — the things these guys have said about God were not true. Yet God gave them a chance to be forgiven and He accepted Job's prayers for them. God is so forgiving. He always gives us the chance to turn away from our sinful ways, and turn back to Him!

During all his suffering, Job never turned away from God. God knew that Job still served Him with his whole life.

THINK IT OVER

Could God call you His servant, living to please Him instead of just yourself? Will you tell God how sorry you are for disobeying Him and start living His way again?

👁 **Read verses 10–17**
- ▷ How did Job's new wealth compare with before? (Job 1 v 3)
- ▷ What else did God do for Job?

When Job had his family, possessions and health taken away from him, his friends said God was punishing him. He must have done a terrible sin. But God let everyone know this wasn't true by giving Job so many blessings. God showed that He loved Job and was pleased that Job hadn't turned away from Him.

God loves His children. Sometimes they go through times of suffering, but God never leaves them. And one day He will give them the best blessing ever – a perfect life with Him.

PRAY ABOUT IT

Talk to God about issues, questions, confessions, challenges and praise that have come from reading Job.

➔ **TAKE IT FURTHER**

The final word on Job – page 121.

Church – what does it do?

In *Essential*, we take time out to explore key truths about God, the Bible and Christianity. This issue, church is under the spotlight. What does the church actually do?

It's a privilege to be part of the church. Sometimes serving alongside other Christians can have its frustrations but it really is mind-blowing to be involved. Christians are chosen by God. Called to follow the Creator of the universe. Adopted into a family who all share the same heavenly Father. And given a wonderful purpose in life to carry out together. Awesome! But what exactly is that purpose? What is the church designed to do?

The church isn't a mere social club. Or holy huddle. It is a living and growing, Jesus-centred community where three things should happen:

THE CHURCH LOVES GOD

The first role of the church is to fall ever deeper in love with God, who loves us beyond measure. That will involve studying the Bible so we can get to know Him better; thanking God for His generosity and grace; singing songs that remind us how great He is (Colossians 3 v 16); and talking to Him in prayer (Ephesians 6 v 18). We praise Him for who He is and what He's done. And we do that in His company as, amazingly, He has promised to be there whenever we meet together (Matthew 18 v 20).

As these things take place, we'll be gradually transformed to be more like Jesus and become increasingly holy and increasingly united (Philippians 2 v 1–2). One day we will meet Jesus face to face — after that, we'll spend forever praising God in the perfection of eternal life. Biggest. Party. Ever.

THE CHURCH LOVES ONE ANOTHER

We're called to love each other
(2 Thessalonians 1 v 3). That involves
practical action as we share what we
have with other Christians in need
(1 John 3 v 16–17). And it involves
encouraging each other to become
more mature in our faith (Colossians
1 v 28). We do that by using our God-
given gifts; whether they are gifts
of teaching, encouraging, serving
or hospitality (1 Corinthians 12 v 28
/ Romans 12 v 6–8), to point each
other to Jesus in word and action.

The church exists to spur one another
on to love and good works (Hebrews
10 v 24) so that when we each reach
the end of our lives we'll be able to
echo Paul: *"I have fought the good
fight, I have finished the race, I have
kept the faith"* (2 Timothy 4 v 7).

THE CHURCH LOVES NON-CHRISTIANS

Thirdly, the church exists to reach out to
those who don't know the good news
of Jesus. To *"go and make disciples of
all nations, baptising them in the name
of the Father and of the Son and of
the Holy Spirit, and teaching them to
obey"* everything Jesus has commanded
(Matthew 28 v 19–20).

This mission involves reflecting the
love of God by caring for others, even
those we don't like very much (Luke
6 v 35–36)! Being willing to answer
questions that people have about
Christianity (1Peter 3 v 15). And by
actively seeking opportunities to show
people what God's rescue plan is all
about (Ephesians 5 v 15–16). This
will bring suffering and opposition
(Philippians 1 v 29–30) but it's
essential work.

People need to hear about Jesus if
they are to follow Him. People can
only be forgiven and gain eternal life
if they respond to the message of the
cross. Being part of this mission is the
most important activity any human
being can be involved in.

**It's exciting stuff. And there's a
role for everyone. So why not chat
to your youth leader or minister
and get more involved in these
three great tasks? Doing so will
transform your life and the lives
of the people around you!**

60 Galatians: Freedom fighters

Back to Galatia, and false teachers had persuaded the Christians there that they had to obey Jewish law to be right with God. Paul said it's all about Jesus, not keeping rules. After all, it's a family business.

👁 Read Galatians 3 v 26–29

ENGAGE YOUR BRAIN

▶ What are we if we trust in Jesus? (v26)

▶ Who is this true for? (v28)

▶ What else are we? (v29)

Take this in. If you trust in Jesus' death to rescue you from sin, you're God's child. It doesn't matter where you're from, what you've done in the past or whether you're male or female. If you trust in Jesus, you're part of the family and will inherit God's amazing promises.

👁 Read Galatians 4 v 1–7

▶ What were we before? (v1–3)

▶ What did God do about this? (v4–5)

▶ Who else did God send? (v6)

▶ What's all that mean for us? (v7)

God gives all Christians the Holy Spirit, who lives in their lives and helps them be close to God, their Father. Like a little child who relies on their daddy (v6).

Christians have been rescued by Jesus. So they're no longer ruled by sin. They are now God's children. And they will inherit God's great gift of life with Him (v7).

PRAY ABOUT IT
Use these verses to thank God for what He's done for you by sending Jesus and His Holy Spirit.

THE BOTTOM LINE
Christians are children of God who are guaranteed a great inheritance.

→ TAKE IT FURTHER
No *Take it further* today.

61 | No u-turn

Yesterday Paul told the Galatians how they'd been rescued by Jesus; they were now God's children; they had the Holy Spirit helping them serve God. Brilliant. So what's the problem?

Read Galatians 4 v 8–11

ENGAGE YOUR BRAIN
- What were they like before? (v8)
- What should they be like now? (v9)
- But what's happened? (v9–10)

Jesus had rescued these Galatian guys from their sinful lives. Surely they would never go back to the way they lived before. That would be stupid. But that's exactly what they've done. They were going back to their old sinful way of trying to earn forgiveness by living good lives. But following Jewish rules and keeping Jewish festivals wouldn't make them right with God. They needed to trust in Jesus' death for them.

THINK IT OVER
- Write down three things you keep doing that displease God?

1.
2.
3.

It's really hard to break your old habits, even when you've become a Christian. Don't worry, it doesn't mean you're not a Christian. But we should still try to beat these sins. We need God to help us kick these habits.

And we must make sure we're not relying on our own efforts to satisfy God. We must trust in Jesus' death in our place to put us right with God. And when we do live God's way, recognise it's the Holy Spirit working in our lives. It's all down to God.

PRAY ABOUT IT
Any idea what you need to talk to God about today?

THE BOTTOM LINE
Don't turn back!

→ TAKE IT FURTHER
Don't turn around; head straight for page 121.

62

Where's your joy?

These Christians in Galatia used to serve God with their whole lives. But they were starting to go back to their old sinful ways. So Paul blasted them...

👁 Read Galatians 4 v 12–16

▷ What was great about the their welcome to Paul? (v13–14)

▷ What had changed? (v15)

▷ How did they now treat Paul? (v16)

THINK IT OVER

▷ Would your friends say you're full of joy?

▷ Why / why not?

▷ Have you lost some of your enthusiasm about your faith?

▷ If so, why do you think that is?

👁 Read verses 17–20

▷ What were the false teachers trying to do? (v17)

▷ How does Paul feel about it all? (v19–20)

Paul cared so much for these believers, he hated seeing them throw their faith away and turn back to their old ways. Once we're set free by Jesus, we must stay free.

Sometimes we can be influenced by enthusiastic ("zealous") people who dazzle us with their words but pull us away from Jesus. Watch out!

PRAY ABOUT IT

Paul wanted Christ to be "formed" in these believers. For them to become more and more like Jesus. What a great thing to aim for. Pray this for yourself and for five Christians you know.

→ TAKE IT FURTHER

Joyfully, er, skip over to page 121.

63 | Children of promise

Paul is determined to show the Galatians how pointless it is to rely on law-keeping to get right with God. This time he uses an Old Testament story to make his point.

👁 Read Galatians 4 v 21–27

Isaac

God had promised Abraham a son, but Sarah had never been able to have children. So when she gave birth to Isaac it was a miracle! That's like God's gift of Jesus. A miracle from God to make us His children.

Ishmael

Abraham had been impatient, and not trusted God's promise. Instead, he had a son (Ishmael) with Hagar, Sarah's maid. That's like us relying on our own efforts to save us. It makes us slaves like Ishmael.

👁 Read verses 28–31

ENGAGE YOUR BRAIN

▶ *So how does this story apply to the Galatians, and to us?*
v28:
v31:

▶ *What can believers expect in life? (v29)*

All Christians are God's children. And they are "children of promise" because God has kept His promise to send Jesus to rescue His people. And just as Ishmael was bullied, Christians face opposition — especially from "religious" people. Yet God's gift of eternal life isn't for law-keeping religious types. It's only for those who trust in Jesus' forgiveness. They're God's children and will receive their eternal inheritance.

THINK IT OVER

▶ *How has v21–31 helped your outlook on life?*

PRAY ABOUT IT

Thank God for His amazing gift to us of Jesus Christ. Ask Him to help Christians you know cope with any hassle they get for following Jesus.

THE BOTTOM LINE

Christians are children of promise.

→ TAKE IT FURTHER

A tiny bit more is on page 121.

64 Do it yourself?

Are you a "do-it-yourself" kind of person? You'll try to fix anything? Or do you prefer to leave it to the experts? Paul says there are some things we can't do ourselves — we must hand them over to the Expert.

👁 Read Galatians 5 v 1–6

ENGAGE YOUR BRAIN

▶ What message is Paul still blasting us with? (v1)

▶ What marks out true believers? (v5–6)

Christians have been set free by Jesus — we don't have to earn our way into heaven. We must trust in God's grace and forgiveness, not ourselves. Otherwise we risk falling away from Jesus (v4). If we have faith in Jesus, it will be shown by our love for others (v6). God gives us the Holy Spirit to help us have faith and show love.

👁 Read verses 7–12

▶ Why were these guys going back to their old ways? (v7–9)

▶ What would happen to these false teachers? (v10)

False preachers had told these Christians that trusting in Jesus wasn't enough. They had to be circumcised too. This was completely untrue, but the Galatians fell for it. Just as a tiny bit of yeast goes through the whole batch of dough, these lies had affected all of the Christians in Galatia. They were no longer trusting in Jesus.

Only trusting in Jesus can put us right with God. You can't add extra rules to that great message! Paul was so furious with these evil preachers that he wished they would chop off their own testicles (v12)!

PRAY ABOUT IT

Ask God to help you understand what it means to trust Jesus. Ask Him to help you show more love for the people around you. And pray that you will see through any lies people tell you about Jesus.

→ TAKE IT FURTHER

Run over to page 121.

65 | Free to love

Paul says that being a Christian means experiencing freedom. Freedom from guilt and God's punishment. But hold on, Christianity = freedom? Really? Do you believe this? Does your life give this impression?

👁 Read Galatians 5 v 13–15

ENGAGE YOUR BRAIN

▷ *How shouldn't we use our freedom? (v13)*

▷ *So how should we use it? (v13–14)*

▷ *How were the Galatians misusing their freedom? (v15)*

Jesus has rescued us from sin. We're free! Yet we so often abuse our freedom. We do whatever pleases us. And instead of encouraging other Christians and working with them for the gospel, we argue and fight and discourage them. That's what these believers were doing.

THINK IT OVER

▷ *How do you misuse your freedom?*

▷ *Which believers do you argue with or undermine or gossip about?*

Instead of using our freedom to indulge in sin, we can serve each other. Show love to other believers. Try to love others as much as we love ourselves.

GET ON WITH IT

▷ *Who can you serve/help?*

▷ *How exactly will you do that?*

▷ *Which believers do you need to be more loving towards?*

▷ *So what are you going to do about that?*

PRAY ABOUT IT

Pray about today's topics, asking for help and thanking God for true freedom in Christ.

THE BOTTOM LINE

Don't abuse your freedom.

→ TAKE IT FURTHER

Feel free to go to page 122.

66 | Spiritual battle

As Christians, we've been set free from sin. But we still battle against it daily. So how do we fight sin?

👁 Read Galatians 5 v 16–18

ENGAGE YOUR BRAIN
▶ *How is the battle described? (v17)*

▶ *What help do we have in the battle against sin? (v16, 18)*

Christians hear two voices. We should always listen to and obey God's voice. That's the Holy Spirit, who lives in every Christian. But our sinful nature sometimes shouts so loudly that we give in and disobey God.

THINK IT OVER
▶ *If we listen to our sinful nature, what kinds of things do we do?*

👁 Read verses 19–21

GET ON WITH IT
Look up the definitions of any of these you're not sure about.
▶ *Below, list the ones you really struggle with:*

▶ *For each one you've listed, write something practical you can do to fight it:*

You can't tackle these things on your own. The Holy Spirit helps Christians in their battle against sin. Whether it's sexual sin (v19), putting other things ahead of God (v20), or sinning in our relationships (v20–21) — God will help us in our fight.

PRAY ABOUT IT
Say sorry to God for those sins you keep falling into. Ask for His Spirit to help you fight these things. It will be a long battle, and sometimes you'll fail, but God's Spirit will win in the end!

→ TAKE IT FURTHER
Battle on to page 122.

67 ¦ Fresh fruit

Yesterday we looked at things Christians really shouldn't do — the sins we battle against. We can only fight them with the help of the Holy Spirit. Today, Paul tells us the positive qualities the Spirit helps Christians to have.

👁 Read Galatians 5 v 22–23

ENGAGE YOUR BRAIN

▶ Which of these qualities do you need more of in your life?

▶ Why?

This is how God wants us to live. Love, joy and peace should be our natural responses to God's love for us and the peace and joy we receive — through Jesus — as God's forgiven children. We should be patient, kind and good towards other people, showing God's love in the way we interact with them.

God expects us to be faithful to Him, gentle to others and showing self-control — fighting sin and temptation. This all sounds brilliant but impossible. We can't become like this by ourselves but the Holy Spirit helps us, making us more like Jesus.

👁 Read verses 24–26

▶ What's true about each Christian's past? (v24)

▶ What's the way forward? (v25)
▶ What must we avoid? (v26)

When we tuned to Jesus, we "crucified" the way we used to live. We turned our back on our sinful self-centredness. So... don't go back and revive it. Instead, keep up with God's Spirit. Co-operate with Him. Do what pleases Him, as He works in us to help us win the battle against sin.

GET ON WITH IT

Read through Galatians 5 v 16–26.
▶ What encourages you?

▶ What's hit you hard?

▶ What do you need to change?

PRAY ABOUT IT

Pray about those things, asking God to help you by His Spirit.

→ TAKE IT FURTHER

Get one more of your five a day on page 122.

READING Galatians 6 v 1–5

68 | Heavy weight

You might have noticed that Christians are not perfect! Our old sinful nature often tempts us to do wrong again. When we realise how much we've let God down, we can feel completely weighed down by sin.

So what can we do? And what if we think a friend is doing stuff they shouldn't?

👁 Read Galatians 6 v 1–2

ENGAGE YOUR BRAIN

ⓘ *What's the advice if a Christian friend is struggling with sin?*

We're in it together! Christians should help each other fight sin. When another Christian is struggling, help them out. Gently. Don't go gossiping to other people. Talk to him/her about it. Pray with them. But be careful not to be tempted into sin yourself.

And when you have sin struggles, make sure you turn to Christian friends and youth leaders for help. It may be embarrassing to admit stuff, but it's much easier to keep going when we've got friends looking out for us.

👁 Read verses 3–5

ⓘ *What attitude must we avoid?*

ⓘ *What practical thing can we do to avoid sin? (v4–5)*

Do you look down on anyone? If someone is struggling more than us, it doesn't mean we're better than them. We're responsible for our own sin. Test yourself regularly. Should I be watching this? Am I showing love to this person? Should I be doing this?

GET ON WITH IT

ⓘ *Which friend do you need to help out?*
ⓘ *Who will you turn to for help with your sin problems?*
ⓘ *Who do you look down on and how will you change?*
ⓘ *How can you test yourself this week?*

PRAY ABOUT IT

Talk to God about each of your answers, thanking Him that the Holy Spirit can help you with these things.

→ TAKE IT FURTHER

Weight for it... page 122.

69 | First-class service

Sin can weigh us down, but God gives us His Holy Spirit and other believers to help us carry the load. Now for some more top tips on how to live for God.

👁 Read Galatians 6 v 6

ENGAGE YOUR BRAIN

▷ *Who teaches you about God's word?*

This verse means that a church should pay its minister's wages. Bible teachers shouldn't have to live in poverty. Christians have a responsibility for their teachers.

👁 Read verses 7–8

▷ *Put these verses into your own words:*

Get the message? We can't fool God. There's no point saying you're a Christian if you don't live for God. People who only serve themselves are heading for destruction. Those who trust Jesus and put Him first are heading for eternal life.

👁 Read verses 9–10

▷ *Why should we "do good"?*

▷ *What makes you "weary in doing good"?*

Living for God means serving others, especially other believers. Even when it's boring or tiring or unappreciated. We should never tire of helping people out — we're serving God!

GET ON WITH IT

▷ *Which of these things will you do this week?*
- *visit an elderly person*
- *offer to baby-sit*
- *do loads of cleaning at home*
- *give to charity*
- *help at a church club*
- *spend time with a lonely person*

PRAY ABOUT IT

Do you really want to serve God by putting other people first? Then ask Him to help you do it this week, and to keep doing it.

→ TAKE IT FURTHER

Second service on page 122.

70 | What's the point?

It's the end of the letter. Paul stops dictating and writes the last bit himself. As if he were writing a persuasive essay, Paul sums up all the main points at the end. Don't miss them.

👁 Read Galatians 6 v 11–18

ENGAGE YOUR BRAIN

▷ *Why were false teachers persuading Christians to get circumcised? (v12)*

▷ *Did these men keep the law themselves? (v13)*

These infiltrators were trying to water down the gospel for fear of their fellow (non-Christian) Jews. They wanted to be accepted socially. So they demanded these Gentile Christians got circumcised.

▷ *What mattered most to Paul? (v14)*

▷ *What's Paul's big point? (v15)*

Being a Christian isn't about feeling good or making friends. It's not all about following rules. It's all about **Jesus**. It's about Jesus dying on the cross, to take the punishment we deserve. It's about trusting Him to forgive our sins and put us right with God. It's about being **changed** by Jesus, so that we now live for God and not for ourselves!

GET ON WITH IT

▷ *What has God taught you through Galatians?*

▷ *How has He encouraged you?*

▷ *What do you need to change?*

PRAY ABOUT IT

Read through the whole letter in one go, talking to God as you do so.

THE BOTTOM LINE

What counts is a new creation — lives changed by and for Jesus Christ.

→ TAKE IT FURTHER

There's no *Take it further* today, so you have extra time to read the whole of Galatians. Go on, try it!

71 Psalms: Living God's way

It's the big one. The longest chapter in the Bible. Psalm 119 is an epic song to God. 176 verses all about God's word and His commands (AKA decrees, precepts, statutes etc). It's so long we're going to take 3 days to sing it.

👁 Read Psalm 119 v 1–16

ENGAGE YOUR BRAIN

▶ How can young people walk God's way? (v1, 9)

▶ What else?
v10:
v11:

▶ How should believers feel about living God's way?

👁 Read verses 17–32

▶ How does the writer feel about himself? (v19, 25, 28)

▶ What does he ask for? (v22–23)

▶ What else? (v27)

▶ How is he determined to live? (v30–32)

👁 Read verses 33–48

PRAY ABOUT IT
Go through v33–40, verse by verse,

putting it into your own words. Use it as a prayer to God. Only say it if you really mean the words.

👁 Read verses 49–64

▶ What's getting the writer down? (v51, 53, 61)

▶ Where does he find comfort and hope? (v49–52)

▶ If we're thankful to God, what should we do? (v62, 63)

If we want to live God's way, we must study, learn and obey His word, the Bible. Our sin means we won't always obey God, but His Spirit keeps changing us. And He sent His Son Jesus to rescue us from the punishment for sin.

PRAY ABOUT IT
Sing your own song to God.

→ TAKE IT FURTHER
More great stuff on page 123.

72 | God's great word

Have you ever wandered away from God? Ever let life get you down? Ever wish you obeyed God more or read the Bible more? Ever need guidance? If you said yes to any of those, this is the psalm for you.

👁 Read Psalm 119 v 65–88

ENGAGE YOUR BRAIN

▷ *What had happened to this guy? (v67–70)*

▷ *What was his attitude to tough times? (v71)*

▷ *What is his prayer? (v76–78)*

▷ *What does he long for? (v81)*

If we've wandered away from God, we can still turn back to Him. When life is hard, we can always ask God for help. If we take His word seriously and obey it, we'll start walking God's way again. Just like this guy, everyone needs salvation. Everyone needs to turn to Jesus for rescue from sin.

👁 Read verses 89–104

▷ *Write down three things we learn about God in these verses:*

- •
- •
- •

This is mind-blowing stuff. God made the earth and that has lasted. But

God's word has always been true and perfect and will be for ever. And His faithfulness will never end — we can rely on God's promises. He'll never let you down.

👁 Read verses 105–120

▷ *Where should we turn for guidance in life? (v105)*

▷ *When we're scared, where should we turn for security? (v114)*

The Bible shows us the best way to live — God's way. When we have decisions to make or life is too much for us, we can turn to God for guidance, help and protection.

PRAY ABOUT IT

Do that right now. Tell God about your current situation. Ask Him for guidance and help. And ask Him to teach you through His word.

→ TAKE IT FURTHER

More mind-blowing stuff on page 123.

73 | Let's pray

The writer of Psalm 119 didn't just say a super-quick prayer and then rush for his breakfast! He had something to ask God that he really needed the Lord to answer. See how he went about it.

👁 Read verses 121–144

ENGAGE YOUR BRAIN

▶ What did he see happening around him? (v126, 136)

▶ What did he think of God's word? (v129, 137–144)

▶ What is his prayer? (v132–135)

👁 Read verses 145–160

▶ How would you describe this guy's prayers? (v145–149)

▶ What does he pray about? (v153–154)

▶ What else does he do in his prayer? (v156, 160)

His prayers were not a bored, quiet mumble. He put his heart into it. He was so desperate for God to hear Him that He even got up in the night to pray! He knew he didn't deserve an answer from God. But he knew how incredibly kind and loving God is. God loves us and answers our prayers!

👁 Read verses 161–176

He couldn't keep quiet about God and about God's word! That's why he wrote this huge, long psalm. He just had to praise God. He wanted everyone to know how much he loved God's word. And he wanted them to love it too.

THINK IT OVER

▶ What do you love talking about to anyone who'll listen?

▶ How often do you talk about what you've read in the Bible?

PRAY ABOUT IT

Pray that you'll be excited about God and His word and that you'll talk to everyone about it. And ask God to help your prayers be more genuine, urgent and full of praise.

→ TAKE IT FURTHER

Now let's look at that surprising last verse. On page 123.

Malachi

The big comeback

It's around 450BC, in Jerusalem. God's people are hungry and disillusioned. There has been no harvest and God seems distant. Over a hundred years earlier, the Lord punished His people for constantly disobeying Him and rejecting Him. God allowed them to be conquered and carried away to Babylon. 70 years later, they were suddenly freed and allowed to return to Jerusalem. They were excited and full of hope. And they rebuilt God's temple.

But now the enthusiasm has gone. They're tired of waiting. Where has God gone? Has He forgotten His people? Does He care about them any more? And why doesn't He do anything about the wicked people who seem to get away with murder?

Malachi (his name means "my messenger") spoke God's message to His disillusioned people. To people who had given up on God and living for Him. To people who doubted God's justice. They didn't doubt God existed; they simply didn't think He was worth following. Why bother?

Christians in the 21st-century can be just the same. They start out their new life with God full of excitement. Prayer is great, the Bible is so exciting, church rocks. Their friends notice a big difference in their lives.

As time passes, enthusiasm wears off. It's hard work living for Jesus. Is it really worth the hassle? Non-Christian friends seem to be doing well without God. Why bother?

Ever felt that way? In Malachi, we'll hear God's message to His dejected Old Testament people. It's also God's message to jaded Christians today. It's a message of warning and hope. It's a message full of God's love. And it's a call to return to living God's way.

In the end

Staggering through a blizzard, it's hard to imagine ever wearing flip flops again. But the day to sun tan your toes will come. God's promises are surer than summer following winter — even if it takes some time.

👁 Read Malachi 1 v 1–3

ENGAGE YOUR BRAIN

🔹 *What do God's people think about His love? (v2)*

God's first words to His people are to remind them of His love. His special, long-term, intimate care for His people — not for everyone, but for them. He had chosen them, just as He'd chosen Jacob and not Esau.

God had disciplined His people, but not abandoned them. He still loved them! God had committed Himself to care for them and would continue to do so.

👁 Read Malachi 1 v 4–5

🔹 *How does God view Edom's reconstruction plans?*

🔹 *What will God demonstrate to Israel?*

While Israel suffered, the future looked bright for Edom. But they were forgetting one thing. God had spoken. And God keeps His promises.

THINK IT THROUGH

People who reject God might talk up their future plans, but they always end in tears. Being loved by God doesn't guarantee a cosy life, but His promises for our future are unbreakable.

PRAY ABOUT IT

Where does life look bleak at the moment? Have you questioned why God doesn't make things better? Be honest with God about your struggles. And declare your faith in His promises, no matter how long the pain lasts.

→ TAKE IT FURTHER

Why are some people not chosen? Find out if God is fair on page 123.

75 | Because I'm worth it

Name your ultimate dinner guest. Someone you admire enough to make you clean the house, dress well and cook like a chef. Ready to roll out the red carpet?

👁 Read Malachi 1 v 6–10

ENGAGE YOUR BRAIN

▷ *How are the priests treating the Lord?*

▷ *What's wrong with their sacrifices?*

▷ *What radical solution does God suggest? (v10)*

The priests' actions suggest they respect God less than they do their dads and bosses. He would rather cancel their entire worship programme than keep putting up with their insults.

👁 Read Malachi 1 v 11–14

▷ *What kind of honour does God deserve? (v11)*

▷ *In what way were people cheating? (See the standard set in Deuteronomy 15 v 21.)*

If you cut corners at work or school, you're assuming that your manager/tutor is too stupid to notice or care. It's a slap in the face to the one in charge. Half-hearted worship cheats God of what He deserves.

THINK IT THROUGH

If we can imagine offering the VIP treatment to royalty, celebrities or heroes, how much more do we owe ultimate honour to the King of everything?

PRAY ABOUT IT

Do you ever treat prayer, church and living to please God like an annoying duty? Confess it now to our gracious King. Ask that today, with His help, your life will bring Him honour.

→ TAKE IT FURTHER

What kind of respect does God want? Check the Bible's blueprint on page 124.

76 | Get out!

Hit 'em where it hurts! Part of the punishment for disgraced sports stars, politicians and medics is to ban them from their professions. Being robbed of their means of money and reputation is a painful penalty.

👁 **Read Malachi 2 v 1–3**

ENGAGE YOUR BRAIN

The job description of a priest included blessing the people and keeping them clean before God.

▶ *What will God do to their blessings?*

▶ *What would being "carried off" mean for their life and work?*

God is holy. Sacrificial worship made this obvious — clean and unclean (holy and unholy) things were kept completely separate. So you can see, an unclean priest was totally useless: an embarrassment to everyone.

👁 **Read Malachi 2 v 4–9**

Levi and his descendants were chosen by God to serve God's people by doing the sacrifice stuff at the temple.

▶ *How had these priests failed in their duties? (v7–8)*

▶ *What were the consequences? (v9)*

These Old Testament priests were expected to lead people to God. The New Testament says that's what every Christian should do.

The great news for us is that we're blessed and made clean by one permanent and perfect Priest—Jesus! (Check out for yourself how superior He is in Hebrews 10 v 10–14.)

PRAY ABOUT IT

Thank God for Christian leaders you know who lead godly lives and aren't afraid to explain God's truth clearly.

→ **TAKE IT FURTHER**

Ready to join the priesthood? See the job description on page 124.

77 | Faith breakers

"I'll always love you, Teddy!" declared the boy each night before turning off the light. But 10 years later, the same stuffed toy would be found squashed in a mouldy box in the shed. Do all promises lose their value with time?

👁 Read Malachi 2 v 10–12

ENGAGE YOUR BRAIN
- ▷ *What has Judah (God's people) done wrong? (v11)*
- ▷ *What will happen to the culprit? (v12)*

From the moment they entered the promised land with Joshua, God commanded His people not to marry foreigners. Why? Other nations had other gods — the Lord wanted His people to stay following Him (Deuteronomy 7 v 3). God's not against interracial marriage. But He is against choosing a partner who isn't a Christian, one of His people. Why? Because it will inevitably compromise our relationship with God. Malachi calls such action "breaking faith" or "being unfaithful".

👁 Read verses 13–16
- ▷ *Why wouldn't God accept their offerings? (v14)*
- ▷ *Why did God make marriage special? (v15)*

- ▷ *What command is repeated in v15 and 16?*

God expected commitment from His people — to be His holy (separate) people; and to commit to each other in marriage. But these guys thought they could do their bit at the temple and then live as they pleased, with no commitment to God. That's unfaithfulness. God has always been faithful, and that's what He requires of us.

The rest of the world might like the idea that commitments get tired and worn out, but not God. He expects us to stay faithful to Him and to our marriage vows too.

PRAY ABOUT IT
Are you considering giving up on something God commands? Pray for His protection against breaking faith.

→ TAKE IT FURTHER
There's even more on page 124.

78 | Fear factor

The people of Judah thought God had stopped caring for them and wasn't worth living for any more. What was their evidence? Well, just look at the world around us...

👁 Read Malachi 2 v 17

ENGAGE YOUR BRAIN

▶ What was the people's cynical, wrong attitude?

▶ How do people you know express such views today?

"What's the point in living for God? Anyone can see non-Christians have a better time." "How can there be a God when the world is so evil?"

▶ How might you answer questions like those?

👁 Read Malachi 3 v 1–5

▶ Who do you think are the two people mentioned in v1?

In the New Testament, John the Baptist announced the arrival of God. Then Jesus came, bringing God's judgment. One day He'll carry out that worldwide judgment once and for all.

Sure, things happen in God's world

that He's opposed to. But don't be fooled into thinking He doesn't care, or won't act. Verses 2–5 explain what His judgment will be like.

▶ How thorough will it be? (v2)

▶ Who will come under God's judgment? (v3, 5)

God demands that people fear Him — honour Him with the way they live. God sent His Son, Jesus the Judge into the world. Those who trust in His death and resurrection will be accepted by God. Those who reject Jesus will be punished when Jesus returns on the day of judgment. Malachi's message is clear — sort your lives out; fear the Lord.

PRAY ABOUT IT

Say sorry to God for any wrong words or attitudes you've directed towards Him. Ask Him to help you live your life with a healthy fear of Him.

→ TAKE IT FURTHER

More questions on page 124.

79 Giving to God

God doesn't change — He's always faithful. Despite centuries of being slapped in the face, God still wanted His people to know Him and His care — and to live for Him.

Read Malachi 3 v 6–12

ENGAGE YOUR BRAIN

- What was God's promise to His disobedient people? (v7)
- What was God's criticism? (v8–9)
- What did God promise if they obeyed Him? (v10–12)

God's people were expected to give Him a "tithe" — a tenth of all they earned. But this lot couldn't be bothered to do even that. Yet not only did God not destroy them, He gave them the chance to turn back to Him and have a bright future.

For us, living after Jesus, the New Testament promises God will care for us, look after our needs — and even make us like Jesus. And we've got eternal life to look forward to.

Read verses 13–18

- What complaints did they make?
  v14:
  v15:

- But what about people who lived God's way? (v16–18)

These guys (v13–15) had loads of excuses for not giving their lives, money and service to God. "It's pointless." "What's in it for me?" "Sinful people seem to get rich." They'd forgotten all that God had done for them. And they'd forgotten His promise of a perfect future for those who stayed faithful to God.

THINK ABOUT IT

- What wrong attitudes do you have about obeying God?
- What will you do about it?

PRAY ABOUT IT

Thank God for all He's done for you — even giving His Son to die for you. Ask Him to help you give more of your time, money, love and obedience to Him.

→ TAKE IT FURTHER

Give in and go to page 124.

80 | Big finish

In Malachi's time, many people just didn't see the point in living God's way — He seemed so distant. OK, so nothing has really changed — people still ignore God. This short book now ends with a big warning and a big promise.

👁 Read Malachi 4 v 1–3

ENGAGE YOUR BRAIN
▶ When Jesus returns, what will happen to arrogant people who ignore God? (v1)
▶ But what will that day be like for believers? (v2)

The Lord may seem distant or non-existent to many people — but the day will come when He will be very real to them as they face the punishment they've earned. That same day of judgment will be a glorious day for believers. It will be the end of suffering and pain and sin in their lives. The sun will dawn on a new eternity of righteousness, healing and perfection. They will celebrate!

👁 Read verses 4–6

▶ What does God want everyone to do? (v4)
▶ Who did He promise to send? (v5)

But Elijah had been dead for many years! The New Testament tells us this

"Elijah" was actually John the Baptist. He would bring the same message as Elijah: "Turn back to God!", and he would prepare the way for Jesus (see Luke 1 v 11–17; Matthew 11 v 7–14).

Today, God still expects people to turn from their sin and turn to Him — trusting in Jesus' death on their behalf. Turning to God means obeying Him in all aspects of our lives, including mending broken family situations (v6).

GET ON WITH IT
▶ Who do you know who ignores God?
▶ What do you need to get across to them?
▶ What do you need to repent of?

PRAY ABOUT IT
Talk to God openly about what He's put on your heart today and from the whole book of Malachi.

➡ TAKE IT FURTHER
No *Take it further* today.

81 : Pray time

What was the last thing you prayed about? How did God answer? When you pray, do you even expect God to answer? And do you notice when He does?

👁 Read Psalm 120

ENGAGE YOUR BRAIN

▶ What has the writer learned about prayer? (v1)

▶ What did he pray about this time? (v2)

▶ What was in store for his lying enemies? (v3–4)

▶ What else does he tell God about? (v5–7)

The psalm writer is having a terrible time. So he takes his problems to God. He tells God exactly how he feels. He knows God's in control and will hear his prayers.

▶ How can you make sure you turn straight to God when you're in distress?

▶ What do you need to talk to Him about?

▶ Will you expect Him to answer?

👁 Read Psalm 121

▶ Why does the psalm writer turn to God for help?
v2:
v3:
v5–8:

In these two psalms, we get some great tips on how to pray:
1. Turn to God for help.
2. Tell Him exactly what's on your mind and how you feel.
3. Trust Him to answer you.
4. Praise Him.

PRAY ABOUT IT

Now put it into practice.

THE BOTTOM LINE

My help comes from the Lord, the Maker of heaven and earth.

→ TAKE IT FURTHER

For more prayer tips, try page 124.

82 | City ditty

The city of God. In Old Testament times, it was Jerusalem, where God shared His presence with His people. For us, it's the heavenly, new Jerusalem, of which we get a foretaste now before the full reality when Jesus returns.

👁 Read Psalm 122

ENGAGE YOUR BRAIN

▶ *What was David excited about? (v1–2)*

▶ *Why did God's people gather together? (v4)*

▶ *What did David want God's people to experience? (v6–9)*

The New Testament says those who trust in Christ are *already* part of God's city, the heavenly Jerusalem (Hebrews 12 v 22–24). We're already part of God's kingdom. And we have the future reality of living in this perfect city to look forward to.

For now, we meet up with God's people. Not to make sacrifices like these guys did — we remember Jesus' one perfect sacrifice for all time, for us. And we thank Him for it, from the heart.

GET ON WITH IT

▶ *How do you view meeting together with fellow Christians?*

▶ *How will you use those times from now on?*

▶ *What attributes of God will you remember to praise Him for?*

PRAY ABOUT IT

Follow David's pattern in this psalm as you talk to God:

1. Thank God that one day you'll be with Him in His eternal city.
2. Spend time praising God for His greatness.
3. Pray for peace and security among Christians you know, particularly in your church.
4. Pray that God's church will prosper: more and more people becoming Christians — part of His kingdom.

→ TAKE IT FURTHER

The new Jerusalem — page 124.

83 | Proverbs: Walking and talking

Back to Proverbs and the search for wisdom. Remember what true wisdom is? Flick back to Proverbs 1 v 7 for a reminder. It's all about giving God the respect He deserves and living for Him. Walking God's way.

👁 Read Proverbs 4 v 1–9

ENGAGE YOUR BRAIN

▶ *Why is wisdom worth having? (v6–9)*

▶ *What form does it take in v2, 4, and 5?*

▶ *What does this tell us about the importance of words?*

▶ *What kind of words are you feeding your mind with — from TV, internet, friends, books, mags?*

👁 Read verses 10–19

▶ *Just how valuable is wisdom? (v10–13)*

▶ *What does being wise mean we must avoid? (v14–15)*

👁 Read verses 20–27

Proverbs is packed with advice on being wise — how to live God's way. Wise living involves every part of us — our hearts (v23), our words (v24), what we look at (v25), and the path we follow in life (v26–27).

GET ON WITH IT

▶ *What is your heart set on?*

▶ *What ungodly or corrupt talk do you need to cut out?*

▶ *What should you fix your eyes on and what should you stop looking at?*

▶ *How can you make sure you follow God's path?*

PRAY IT THROUGH

Ask God to train you to feed your mind with wise words. And ask Him to help you speak God-wise words to others too.

THE BOTTOM LINE

Guard your heart.

→ TAKE IT FURTHER

No *Take it further* today.

84 | Sex wise

"God's against sex and hates fun." A common view but not an accurate one. Today we meet Ms Sleeparound and are warned from going back to her place. But Proverbs also celebrates the beauty of sex within marriage.

👁 Read Proverbs 5 v 1–14

ENGAGE YOUR BRAIN

▷ *What are Ms Sleeparound's words like? (v3)*

▷ *But what's she really like? (v4–6)*

▷ *How might sleeping around ruin your life?*

▷ *So what should we do? (v8)*

Notice the importance of words again (v1–2). The adulteress happens to be female, but Proverbs isn't being sexist. It's just using the familiar idea of a seductive, tempting woman. Of course, the warnings here are as much for the lasses as the lads. We all face sexual temptation.

👁 Read verses 15–23

▷ *What watery point is being made in v15–20?*

▷ *Who do we answer to — about sex and everything? (v21)*

▷ *What will happen to people who ignore God's orders? (v22–23)*

Of course God isn't against sex — He invented it! And so He designed its boundaries. Sex must be kept within marriage. Why spoil something so beautiful?

THINK IT OVER

▷ *In what other ways do we misuse God's gift of sex?*

▷ *What do you need to change in your life?*

PRAY ABOUT IT

Thank God for creating sex. Ask Him to help you steer clear of Ms or Mr Sleeparound. And to not misuse sex.

Doubtless, you'll be able to think of practical ways you can do this. But will you actually do it?

➔ TAKE IT FURTHER

Naughty thoughts on page 125.

85 Great ant

Today we meet Mr Sluggard (AKA Mr Slob). Well, we'll meet him if he can be bothered to get out of bed. But first, what do you do if you make a promise that you realise you can't actually keep.

👁 Read Proverbs 6 v 1–5

It's a custom from Old Testament times. This guy made a promise to pay his friend's debts if his friend couldn't pay them. Sure enough, his friend couldn't pay, so now he's stuck with the debt and can't pay it.

▷ What should he do? (v3)

A promise is any time you say you'll do something, not just when you use the words "I promise". Sometimes we can be trapped by our own words. Later we realise that we can't keep the promise and have to back down. We should apologise to the person we made the promise to, and humbly ask them to let us off.

👁 Read verses 6–11

▷ What does this slob need to learn? (v6–8)

▷ What's his problem? (v9)

▷ What will it lead to? (v11)

Ever watched an ant at work? To make an ant-hill, each little piece of soil has to be carried by an ant to the top of the mound. That's a huge number of trips up and down. And even though the ant has no boss keeping an eye on it, it doesn't stop until the work is finished. God wants us to use our time wisely. That means working hard. It means doing stuff for other people, not just pleasing ourselves.

GET ON WITH IT
▷ How can you be less lazy?

PRAY ABOUT IT
Ask God to help you keep your promises. And pray that you'll be less slob-like and more ant-like.

→ TAKE IT FURTHER
Get out of bed, lazybones, and go to page 125.

86 | Six seven hate

What are your pet hates? Other people's bad breath? Shopping? Sport? Bad losers? Earwax? Wasps? Today we discover what God's pet hates are.

👁 Read Proverbs 6 v 12–15

ENGAGE YOUR BRAIN

▶ *How is this person described? (v12–14)*

▶ *What will happen to him? (v15)*

God hates lies and deceit. People who live that way — ignoring God and living to please themselves — can expect God's punishment in the end.

👁 Read verses 16–19

▶ *What are God's pet hates?*
-
-
-
-
-
-
-

THINK IT OVER

Haughty eyes means a proud attitude that looks down on other people. Are you ever guilty of that? Do you lie? Have a fiery or violent temper? Plan things you know are wrong? Rush into sin even when you know you shouldn't? Gossip falsely about people? Cause trouble between other Christians?

PRAY ABOUT IT

Talk to God honestly and at length about the things from that list that you find it hard to fight against. Say sorry to God for the times you've done things He hates. Ask Him to help you stop doing those things, and do more of the things He loves.

→ TAKE IT FURTHER

No *Take it further* today, so you have extra time talking to God.

87 | Straight thinking on sex

The way we think affects the way we act. So, if we think sex outside marriage is harmless/fun/OK if you love the person, then sooner or later that will affect the way we behave.

👁 Read Proverbs 6 v 20–35

▶ *What can we do to help ourselves think straight? (v20–24)*

▶ *What are the reasons for avoiding Ms/Mr Sleeparound?*

▶ *Why is sex outside marriage more stupid than stealing bread when you're starving? (v30–35)*

Sex outside marriage is playing with fire. In fact, it's like trying to scoop fire from your lap without being burned. Someone always gets hurt.

👁 Read Proverbs 7 v 1–27

▶ *How might you make similar mistakes to this lad? (v7–20)*

▶ *What tempted him?*
v13:
v14:
v16–17:
v18–20:
v21:

▶ *What kind of things entice you to turn your back on wise living?*

THINK IT OVER

Think about the link between how you think and how you act.

▶ *What affects the way you think about sex?*

▶ *Is it what the Bible says? Or are you listening to what the world around you says about sex?*

▶ *How does this affect the way you behave?*

PRAY ABOUT IT

Don't forget Proverbs 7 v 1–5. Ask God to help you stick to the Bible's wisdom about the beauty of sex within marriage and the stupidity of sex outside marriage.

→ TAKE IT FURTHER

More straight thinking on page 125.

88 | Wisdom for the world

More lessons in being wise today. And not just for "normal" people like us. Even world leaders need to hear these words of wisdom.

👁 Read Proverbs 8 v 1–21

▶ Who needs true wisdom? (v4)

▶ What are truly wise words like? (v6–9)

▶ Why is living wisely more important than getting rich? (v10–11)

▶ Why is godly wisdom vital for world leaders? (v14–21)

Lady Wisdom is inviting the whole world to become God-wise. That means living God's way (and the New Testament tells us that's following Jesus Christ). So we should be like Lady Wisdom when we talk to our friends about Jesus.

👁 Read verses 22–31

▶ What is Wisdom's relationship to God? (v22)

▶ What was Wisdom's role in creation? (v30–31)

Here, Wisdom is someone who was around when God made the universe. The New Testament calls Jesus God's Wisdom — and tells us Jesus was the person through whom God made the world. Incredible.

👁 Read verses 32–36

▶ Why is it so vital, to know Jesus, God's Wisdom? (v35–36)

▶ How often should we listen to Wisdom's words? (v34) And why?

PRAY ABOUT IT

Thank God for Jesus, God's Wisdom. Pray that you'll keep getting to know Jesus better and make Him known to others. And plan to be God-wise each day.

→ TAKE IT FURTHER

A tiny bit more is on page 125.

89 | Serious decision

You've received two party invitations. One to a feast with Lady Wisdom, and one to go to the house of Miss Foolish. It seems like a no brainer...

👁 Read Proverbs 9 v 1–6

ENGAGE YOUR BRAIN

▶ *How much trouble has Wisdom taken over the party? (v1–3)*

▶ *Who's invited? (v4)*

▶ *What does the invitation say? (v5)*

This invitation is to us. We're the simple ones — without God's wisdom, we don't know how to live in God's world.

👁 Read verses 7–12

We all know people who are quick to mock and point out people's faults (maybe you're like that).

▶ *How does this person react when you point out their faults? (v7–8)*

▶ *How does a wise person react? (v8–9)*

▶ *What are we reminded about true wisdom? (v10–12)*

If we take God seriously, we'll want to obey Him. So we should actually be grateful when another Christian helpfully corrects us. That might involve a change of attitude.

👁 Read verses 13–18

▶ *What's Miss Foolish like? (v13)*

▶ *What happens to those who accept her invitation? (v18)*

See who's invited (v16)? Aren't they the same people Lady Wisdom invited? That's us. So, we've got to decide which party to go to. We've got to decide whether or not we'll take God seriously and accept His invitation to live wisely.

PRAY ABOUT IT

Ask God to help you take Him seriously — following Jesus and ignoring any foolish advice you get.

→ TAKE IT FURTHER

Whoosh over to Isaiah on page 125.

90 | Psalms: Songs of ascents

Psalms 123 & 124 are "songs of ascents" — they were sung as God's people travelled up to God's temple in Jerusalem. They're good for Christians now, too. We're on our way to God's new, eternal Jerusalem, to be with Him.

👁 Read Psalm 123

ENGAGE YOUR BRAIN

- ▶ *What kinds of problems did these people face? (v3–4)*
- ▶ *How should believers respond to such troubles? (v1–2)*

Just as slaves trusted their masters' judgment and looked to them for protection and help — that's how this man related to God. He lifted his sights away from the problem, looked to God and prayed for help.

THINK IT OVER

- ▶ *What kind of pressures do you face as a Christian?*
- ▶ *Do you tend to focus on a problem and let it take over?*
- ▶ *Or do you focus on God and take your problems to Him?*

Read Psalm 124

- ▶ *How do v3 and v5 help us picture how hopeless Israel must have felt?*

- ▶ *How trapped were the Israelites? (v6–7)*
- ▶ *What difference did it make that God was on Israel's side?*

THINK IT OVER

- ▶ *Do you live as if God's in control of everything and everyone?*
- ▶ *Really, even when things around us seem out of control?*
- ▶ *What do we learn about God's character in v1–2, 6, 8?*
- ▶ *So why turn elsewhere for help?*
- ▶ *Why turn to God only when you've run out of other options?*

PRAY ABOUT IT

In times of trouble, don't forget what God is like, and that He's the only one to turn to. Take any pressures or problems to Him right now.

→ TAKE IT FURTHER

Go on up to page 125.

91 Surround sound

For the Israelites, the temple at Jerusalem symbolised God living among them. To be there, on Mount Zion, was to be where God was. This psalm was a song for believers who had made their way to Jerusalem.

👁 Read Psalm 125 v 1–2

ⓘ How are God's people described?

ⓘ Do these verses suggest a distant God or one personally involved with His people?

ⓘ How does v2 encourage you?

👁 Read verse 3

Even those who trust God (here called "the righteous") are surrounded by wrong and evil.

ⓘ What then might God's people be tempted to do?

ⓘ What's the warning here for us?

👁 Read verses 4–5

We're to be solid, trusting Christians, like the believers here. They were confident in God and so concerned that His will got done that they could pray verses 4–5. The last words of verse 5 remind us there's peace with God for those who trust Him.

THINK IT OVER

ⓘ Do you trust in the Lord?

ⓘ When are you tempted to give up and behave in the same way as your unbelieving friends?

ⓘ Could you pray verses 4–5 and mean it?

PRAY ABOUT IT

Try to write this psalm in your own words, so that it reflects your situation. Use ideas relevant to your everyday life. Then prayerfully read it to God.

➜ TAKE IT FURTHER

No *Take it Further* today, to give you extra time to write your psalm.

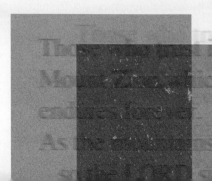

92 | Crying with laughter

Have you ever felt happy and sad at the same time? Life often isn't black and white. There are things to be joyful about and stuff that gets us down. This psalm is full of celebration and yet tinged with tears.

It may have been written when when God's people came back from exile in Babylon. What a moment — getting back to God's city, Jerusalem! But it was immediately followed by a time of depression and disappointment (see Haggai 1 v 5–11). This psalm reflects that mix of emotions.

👁 Read Psalm 126 v 1–3

▶ *How did they feel on returning to Jerusalem? (v1–3)*

▶ *Who was behind it all?*

👁 Read verse 4–6

▶ *How are these verses different?*

Maybe the writer now faced the fact that they were as needy and dependent on God as ever. The new situation brought new worries and challenges. They really needed God's help. As they waited for His help, they were to get on and be obedient to Him. And God would definitely look after them (v5–6).

Christians now can know the excitement of being set right with God through what Jesus has done. Great! But we know there are always hard times, new problems. This psalm says: Lay it all open before God — talk to Him. And keep on living for Him. And He'll more than take care of us.

PRAY ABOUT IT

▶ *What are your expectations of the Christian life?*

▶ *How will you bring them in line with what the Bible says about it?*

Pray about what you've learned in this psalm.

THE BOTTOM LINE

Praise God and keep talking to Him through times of joy and times of tears.

➔ TAKE IT FURTHER

Streams of words on page 125.

TAKE IT FURTHER

MARK
Guess who

1 – GET READY!

Read Hebrews 1 v 1–3

▶ *Why is Jesus so much better than the prophets?*

▶ *Why is it so amazing that God has come in person?*

Read Mark 1 v 8

Check out Old Testament prophets delivering God's promise in **Joel 2 v 28-29** and **Isaiah 44 v 3**. All that's being fulfilled! **Acts chapter 2** documents the historic moment when Jesus gave His Spirit. Ever since, when someone comes to trust in Jesus, they receive God's Spirit to help them live for Him.

2 – BAPTISM, BLESSING & TEMPTATION

Interestingly, the other big mention of the Holy Spirit like a dove comes way back in Genesis 1 v 2, where the Spirit of God literally "flutters" over the waters before creation begins. Jesus coming to earth is as significant as creation itself — it marks the beginning of a new creation... one that will be completed when Jesus returns.

3 – HERE COMES THE KINGDOM

Jesus says to Peter and Andrew that He will make them "fishers of men". He's going to help them draw in people to His kingdom. If you're a Christian, do you see yourself that way? Being an ordinary fisherman is hard work — early starts, long hours, unglamorous, often cold, dark and smelly. Telling people about Jesus can often be tough too — but it's the most wonderful job in the world. Pray now that God would help you fish for people today and every day.

4 – THE HOLY ONE OF GOD

Read Matthew 28 v 18–20

▶ *What big claim does Jesus make? (v18)*

▶ *So how does Jesus want His followers to respond? (v19–20)*

Because of who Jesus is — the crucified, risen Lord, in charge of absolutely everything — He deserves all people to love Him and respect Him. If we understand who Jesus is, we'll love and respect Him so much that we'll tell others about Him. Because we'll want Him to enjoy their love and respect, too. Jesus is Lord — therefore we should tell others about Him. But doing this is hard! That's why the last sentence of Matthew's Gospel is fantastic! Jesus doesn't just send us to tell people about Him — He goes with us as we do it.

5 – MIRACLE MAN

Have you ever wondered why Jesus sometimes tells people to keep quiet about their miraculous healings (v44)? Or why He stops demons from telling people who He is (v34)? In the context of what we've just read, it would seem that huge crowds desperate to catch a glimpse of the newest celebrity hindered Jesus from teaching about God's rescue (see v45). Jesus' popularity as a healer meant that people who wanted to hear Jesus' teaching couldn't get close.

6 – RAISING THE ROOF
Read Psalm 51

Look particularly at verse 4. All our sin is against God. Use this psalm to help you say sorry to God for the things you have said, thought and done that are evil in His sight.

7 – SIN SICKNESS
Read Luke 18 v 9–14

God knows we're not perfect; that's why Jesus came. All He wants is for us to acknowledge our sin and turn to Him for mercy and forgiveness. Self-righteousness is very dangerous because it prevents us getting the help we so desperately need.

8 – FAST AND FURIOUS

Why not learn Philippians 4 v 4–7 by heart? You can find various versions of it set to music if you find that easier. And don't just learn it — do it! Look at the promises in v5 and v7.

9 – AN EAR FOR TROUBLE
Read Matthew 11 v 28–30

This famous saying comes just before the same incident in Matthew's Gospel — that is no coincidence. Why not take some time to learn v28 by heart? It will be of great comfort to you in the future and is a wonderful promise to share with people who don't yet follow Jesus.

10 – WITHERED RELIGION

People often say that Jesus brings unity, and that is true, but He also brings unity between His enemies. The Pharisees and the Herodians in v6 would never usually have worked together, but their mutual hatred of Jesus brings them together. Do you see that in the world around you? People who would normally be enemies ganging up to pour scorn on Jesus and His followers?

11 – JESUS VS EVIL

We don't talk much about spiritual opposition in the western world, but as the film *The Usual Suspects* puts it: "The greatest trick the devil ever pulled was convincing the world he didn't exist" (it's actually originally a quote by a 19th-century French thinker!).

Remember three things when you think about this whole area:
1) Evil spiritual forces are real; the Bible makes that perfectly clear.
2) Jesus defeated them comprehensively at the cross, so we don't need to be frightened.
3) Be alert and wary but know that you're on the winning side.

Check out Ephesians 6 v 10–18, James 4 v 7 and 1 Peter 5 v 8–11.

12 – JESUS VS SATAN

Some Christians worry that they might have inadvertently committed the "unforgivable sin". But Jesus is quite clear, the only thing that is unforgiveable is rejecting our source of forgiveness. If we reject Jesus, we can't be forgiven. If you throw away the lifebelt, you can't be rescued from the shipwreck. Whatever you might have done — lied, cheated, even killed someone — Jesus can and will forgive you if you turn to Him in faith and repentance. Incredible.

13 – THE IN CROWD

If you're the only Christian in your family, take heart from these verses. Jesus faced tough opposition from His nearest relatives (3 v 21). So when your parents or brothers and sisters think you're a "religious nut" or you're "just going through a phase", He understands. But more than that, you have a new family too — Jesus is your brother — see v35. If you are blessed by having an understanding Christian family,

can you share this encouraging truth with someone you know who doesn't have a Christian family?

14 – INSIDE OUT

Look ahead to verses 33–34

▶ *How does Jesus make sure His disciples understand?*

There are many atheist professors of theology. Simply knowing what the Bible says doesn't make you a Christian. We need to know Jesus and come to Him to understand what we read.

▶ *Do you ask for His help every time you read His word?*

15 – GONE TO SEED

▶ *Do you feel discouraged when not many people seem to become Christians?*

▶ *Does this parable help you to see why that might be?*

▶ *Are there people you can pray for who seem like the path, the rocky soil or the soil infested with weeds?*

Ask God to make them good soil — and keep sowing the seed!

16 – SEE HEAR

Have a look at what James has to say about how we should approach God's word in the Bible: **James 1v 22–25.** Pray that God would help you to listen, consider and be changed by what you read in the Bible.

17 – READY, STEADY, GROW!

Check out God's plan for the church —
that small and seemingly insignificant
group of people on earth.

Read Ephesians 3 v 8–11

Then look back at the parables of the
growing seed and the mustard seed.

18 – THAT SINKING FEELING

This Bible bit is not about "the storms of
life". That's not the main point here. But
it is true that knowing this powerful and
loving Jesus will help us when life gets
turbulent. Jesus is God. Don't take Him for
granted, and never forget how powerful
He is. Is there anything you want to say to
Him right now?

JOB

Why me?

19 – SATAN'S TAKEAWAY

Read verses 6–12

Satan means "accuser". Some people get
wrongly worked up about him; others
don't take him seriously enough. In these
verses we see him testing the loyalty of
God's people. But his power is limited.
He's on a chain. Never think that God and
Satan are two equal powers fighting over
the universe. God alone is in charge.

Check out 1 John 3 v 8

Jesus has broken the devil's power.
And how encouraging are **James 4 v 7**
and **1 Peter 5 v 8–9**?

20 – A SORE POINT

Read verses 11–13 again

When a friend is ill or upset, we often
either ignore them or try too hard to cheer
them up. Talking at them or trying to solve
their problems might not be what they
need! It's usually better to keep quiet and
just be with them. Listen to them. Show
them you care. And pray for them.

21 – HAPPY DEATHDAY!

Read 2 Corinthians 12 v 7–10

▶ How did God help Paul to stay humble
and dependent on Him? (v7)
▶ What did Paul ask for? (v8)
▶ What was God's response and why?
▶ Who was really in control? (v9)
▶ When bad or annoying things happen,
do you trust that God is behind all
events for your good?
▶ How should we pray in those sorts of
situations?
▶ How did Jesus pray? (Matthew 26 v
36–45)

Spend time thinking about the difficulties
in your life. Ask God to transform the way
you look at them so that you can depend
more and more on His strength when you
feel weakest.

22 – THE SILENCE IS OVER

Read Job chapter 5

Eliphaz thinks Job has no right to resent
his suffering and is being foolish.

▶ What good points does Eliphaz make
about God?
v9–10:

113

v12–14:

v15–16:

▶ *What's his view of suffering? (v17–26)*

He's right that God is powerful and perfect and that He looks after His people. But Eliphaz is dead wrong that all suffering is God punishing and disciplining us. Job's faith in God was being tested and he still refused to turn against the Lord. Go Job!

23 – FAILING FRIENDS
Read Job chapter 7

▶ *How does Job describe his situation? (v1–5)*

▶ *What is Job determined to do? (v11)*

▶ *What does he ask God to do? (v20–21)*

Job wants to know why God even bothers with such insignificant creatures as humans. Why does God seem so interested in Job? "Why are you always on my back, God???" Yet this constant attention from God shows that He loves Job. God is always watching us humans. We're not insignificant. How could we be if God's interested in us? He created us in His image and He looks out for us. He wants us to turn to Him. He loves us.

24 – BILDAD BLABBERS
Read verses 5–7 again

This is "prosperity gospel" — if you live God's way, He will make you wealthy and healthy. The better you live, the richer you'll be. Sounds good! But it's nonsense. Jesus was born into a far from rich family

and was given an animal trough as His bed. He said that the birds have nests and foxes have holes, but He had nowhere to lay His head (Matthew 8 v 20). He depended on the hospitality of others. And check out Paul's situation...

Read 2 Corinthians 6 v 3–10
The Christian life can be really tough. It can involve serious suffering and persecution. Yet despite that, we can rejoice in knowing God, in having our sins forgiven, in having a wonderful inheritance secure in heaven and in being "in Christ". And we can share those riches with others!

25 – GOD'S GREAT!
Read Job chapter 10

▶ *How does Job view himself?*

▶ *What questions does he ask God?*

▶ *What does he recognise God has done for him?*

▶ *What does he get wrong about God?*

▶ *What does Job long for?*

27 – JOB FIGHTS BACK
Read Job 13 v 20 – 14 v 22

In chapter 14, Job compares a tree that will sprout again even though it's been cut down (v7–9) with the fate of humanity: once cut down, it will be no more (v10–12).

▶ *So what does Job hope for? (v13–17)*

Read Mark 14 v 32–42

▶ *What did Jesus do in response to His suffering?*

Read 2 Corinthians 1 v 8–11

▶ *How did Paul respond to suffering?*

Ask God to help you to place your hope in Jesus when you're suffering, for He's the one who suffered in your place.

Read Psalm 73

Ever wonder if all your non-Christian friends are right and you're wrong? Asaph did. He was looking around at the world instead of looking up to heaven. It's easy to do. We see others seemingly better off and more happy than we are. We start to resent it and doubt God's promises.

▶ *What had caused him to lose his sense of perspective? (v21–22)*

▶ *But what great truths can believers cling on to? (v23–26)*

▶ *How does he compare those who are right with God and those who aren't? (v27–28)*

Everything isn't as it seems. God will punish those who reject Him, however successful they seem. We were all heading for that punishment. But for those of us who've accepted the forgiveness offered by Jesus, the future is far brighter. God holds our hand, guiding us. He's all we need and He's leading us into glory.

Read Job 17 v 11–16

All Job's dreams and hopes seem to have come to a devastating end. He stares death in the face, believing it's the only

true home he'll have, and that it would be a rest from his suffering. And yet... there *is* hope for the believer.

Read 1 Corinthians 15 v 20–28

▶ *Why can believers be confident in the face of death?*

Thank God that He rescues sinners like us from eternal death.

Read Romans 3 v 21–26

▶ *Summarise the good news from these verses in your own words.*

▶ *What does Jesus' death tell us about God?*

How can you use the ideas in this mind-blowing passage to tell your friends about what God has done for sinful people like us? Take time to work out how you can clearly explain this great news. Write it down. Practise it. And then do it.

GALATIANS
Freedom fighters

For the background to the whole Galatian situation, read about Paul's first visit to Galatia in **Acts chapters 13 and 14**.

Read Acts 15 v 1–11

▶ *What do the Jewish believers suggest is necessary to be saved? (v1, v5)*

▶ *What does Peter remind everyone about:*
a) God's choice? (v7)

b) God's gift? (v8)

c) God's work? (v9)

d) God's salvation? (v11)

▶ How is anyone saved? (v11)

34 – FROM PERSECUTOR TO PREACHER

Read Acts chapter 9

▶ Sum up Saul's attitude and behaviour towards Christians in v1–2. (The Way = Christianity)

▶ How does Jesus describe his behaviour? (v4–5)

▶ What's so amazing about Ananias' first words to Saul, considering Saul's past? (v17)

▶ What is Saul's immediate reaction to God's grace? (v20)

▶ What does he preach about Jesus? (v20 and v22)

▶ Has God's grace had the same effect on you?

The good news about Jesus turns enemies into brothers, makes the blind see and transforms persecutors into believers!

35 – IT'S ALL ABOUT JESUS

Check out what Proverbs says about poor and needy people:

Proverbs 14 v 20–21, 31

Proverbs 22 v 1–2, 9, 22–23

▶ How do these proverbs challenge your attitude and actions?

▶ So what will you do about it?

37 – SIN? SO WHAT?

Read verse 20 again
and then Romans 6 v 1–7

Jesus died on the cross to take the punishment we deserve. So when you become a Christian, you have all your wrongs forgiven by Jesus. It's as though your sinful life has died with Jesus. You no longer want to disobey God; you want to please Him. That's the plan, anyway.

Our old self dies when we trust in Jesus and His death in our place. We're born again, freed from the grip sin had on our lives. Free to serve God. Yes, we'll still mess up sometimes, but sin no longer rules us — God does.

38 – YOU FOOLISH GALATIANS!

Read verses 1–5 again

Old Testament law says: "Do this".
The gospel says: "Jesus has done it all".

▶ What rules have people told you to follow in order to be a "real", "serious" Christian?

▶ What's likely to cause you to take your eyes off the gospel?

▶ What in your life would make Paul call you a "foolish" Christian?

39 – CURSED THINGS FIRST

Check out verse 11 again

It's easy to slip into the mindset which thinks we can be acceptable to God through our own efforts and by being "good Christians".

▶ How does this show up in your own life?

ⓘ *What measures can you take to protect yourself from this kind of thinking?*

40 – POINT OF LAW
Slowly read verses 18–24

In just 7 verses, Paul spans about 2000 years: God's promise to Abraham was confirmed by Moses (because the law didn't cancel it but pointed out our need for it) and was fulfilled in Jesus.

ⓘ *How does Paul's explanation help us to understand how the whole Bible fits together?*
ⓘ *What's been God's plan all along?*

PROVERBS
Wise up!

41 – WHY BOTHER WITH PROVERBS?

A large amount of Proverbs was written by King Solomon.

Read 1 Kings 4 v 29–34

ⓘ *How wise was Solomon? (v29–31)*
ⓘ *How did he use this wisdom? (v32–34)*
ⓘ *Where did it come from? (v29)*

42 – MUM'S THE WORD

Read Psalm 1

ⓘ *Who are the two groups of people mentioned in Psalm 1?*
ⓘ *What does the "blessed" person do?*
ⓘ *And what doesn't he do?*

Blessed means favoured by God, happy. People blessed by God want to live His way, not hang out with the wicked,

copying what they do (v1). Instead, God's people fill their minds and hearts with God's law, the Bible. And people who walk God's way are successful! That doesn't mean they'll be millionaires. Much better than that — they'll become more like Jesus.

43 – THE VOICE OF WISDOM
Read 1 Corinthians 1 v 18–31

ⓘ *Write down what Paul says about wisdom:*

•
•
•
•
•
•

45 – LIVE LONG AND PROSPER
Read verses 1–2 and 7–8 again

Are health and wealth guaranteed? Both our experience and New Testament teaching shows this isn't the case, right? So it must be understood in terms of God's new world, when Jesus returns. Only then will freedom from suffering be known.

46 – WHAT WISDOM'S WORTH
Read verses 11–12 and then Hebrews 12 v 4–11

ⓘ *What will our day-to-day Christian life be like?*
ⓘ *Why is this? (v7)*
ⓘ *What should be the result of this? (v10–11)*

God uses tough times in life both to discipline us and help us keep going. Only parents who don't love their children don't discipline them and encourage them in the right way of living. Life as a Christian may be painful at times, but God is constantly training us and making us more like Him.

47 – WISE ADVICE

**Read verse 32 again
and then John 15 v 9–17**

- ▶ *How are we to "remain in" Jesus and His love? (v10)*
- ▶ *What specific command does Jesus give? (v12)*
- ▶ *How did Jesus show His love for us? (v13)*
- ▶ *Can we boast about choosing to follow Jesus?*
- ▶ *Why / why not? (v16)*

If you're a Christian, Jesus chose you. He calls you His friend and He specifically chose you to bear fruit for God — fruit that will last. If you're not excited by that, then you're probably dead!

JOB

48 – WHY ME?

See how Jesus dealt with people like Eliphaz in Matthew 15 v 1–9

- ▶ *What accusation was made? (v2)*
- ▶ *How did Jesus respond? (v3)*
- ▶ *How were these men being hypocritical? (v4–6)*

Jesus pointed out how the Pharisees

made up ridiculous rules that actually stopped people from serving God and honouring their parents! He showed up their "religion" for the sham it was — they were all talk and their hearts were not devoted to God (v8). The Pharisees were focusing on man-made rules. But they weren't concerned about their hearts, their thoughts or their words — the important stuff.

- ▶ *In what ways do you concentrate on keeping rules or appearing good rather than dealing with your evil thoughts?*
- ▶ *What specific stuff do you need God's help to deal with?*

49 – DISTANT DEITY?

Read Job chapter 24

It's the same now as it was then. All over the world, people suffer. Why do these bad things happen? Job's friends say people suffer because God is punishing them for particular things they've done wrong. Not true! God often lets bad things happen so people will turn to Him.

Sometimes it seems as though evil people get away with making others suffer. God *will* punish such people, but in His own time (v22–24). God is totally fair and will punish sin.

50 – GOD'S GREATNESS

Job suffers a lot in his 42 chapters, and he never really understands why. Which raises a big question that many people have:

why does God let bad things happen?

Read Luke 13 v 1–5

Many people thought God was punishing these people for some terrible sin. But Jesus said that's not true. These people were no worse than anyone else. The fact is, we don't always know why bad things happen. Why some people die young, why thousands are killed in wars and disasters. Jesus says the most important thing is to get right with God before you die. To repent — turn away from your wrong ways and ask God to forgive you.

Now read John 9 v 1–3

Sometimes bad things happen so that God can show His greatness. He might heal someone in an amazing way. Or a person in a bad situation might realise that the only one who can help them is God. God often does amazing things in bad situations!

51 – TREASURE HUNT

Read Colossians 2 v 1–7

- ▶ Where is true wisdom found? (v3)
- ▶ If we're truly wise, trusting in Jesus, how should we live? (v6–7)

All the treasures of God are found in Jesus! As Christians grow, they need to continue living Jesus' way, building their lives on Him, becoming strong in their faith. Jesus gives Christians everything they need. He saved them from their sins. He's given them the Bible to teach them, and the Holy Spirit to help them live for

Him! So they should be bursting with thankfulness (v7)!

Thank Jesus that He's all you need. Take some extra time now to thank Him for what He's done in your life.

52 – JOB THE DEFENDANT

The book of Job has been less concerned with giving us an answer for suffering, and more concerned with helping us understand the sovereign nature of God — that He is in complete control, even when we're suffering.

Read 1 Peter 1 v 3–9

- ▶ How should Christians view their suffering? (v6–7)
- ▶ What will be the outcome? (v8–9)
- ▶ So what should we celebrate even in tough times? (v3–6)

53 – ELI-WHO?

Read Job 33 v 23–33

Elihu correctly told Job he needed to ask God to pay the ransom for his sins. To ask God to forgive him, and put an end to his suffering. But, like Job's other friends, Elihu had got things wrong too. Job was already trusting God to provide a ransom for his sins, but that still didn't make him healthy again!

People want to be healthy and wealthy and happy. But that's not the most important thing. It's much more important to be forgiven by God. Only Jesus, by His death on the cross, can pay for our sins.

Read Mark 10 v 45

Now read it again. Meditate on it. That means think about it. Think about what Jesus has done and how that affects you. And then spend time praying about it.

55 – GOD SPEAKS

Read Colossians 1 v 15–20

▶ *Paul is talking about Jesus. How does Paul describe Him in v15?*

▶ *Does anything surprise you in v16–17?*

▶ *Despite being God, what was Jesus prepared to do? (v20)*

In Bible times, the son who was born first got special rights and privileges. He was number one. Jesus is in charge of the whole of creation! He is the Creator of all things and everything was created for Him (v16). He's the one who holds the world together (v17)! Jesus is number one.

56 – CREATURE COMFORT

Read Psalm 104

▶ *What are some of the amazing things God has done?*

v5:

v6–8:

v10–12:

v14–15:

▶ *What is God's relationship with all He has created? (v27–30)*

▶ *What's the purpose of creation? (v31)*

▶ *How should we respond to our awesome God? (v33–34)*

God didn't just create the world and then leave it alone. God is intimately involved in the daily life of all creatures. Our lives depend completely on God — eating, breathing, everything. Someone once said: "The whole purpose of humans is to glorify God and to enjoy Him for ever". Fantastic, isn't it? People are made in God's image and can know God personally. But they're also to blame for turning away from Him (v35).

Next time you're out and about, marvel at the world God's made. Think what this says about God's character. And do the right thing and praise Him for it.

57 – JOB SILENCED

Read Job 40 v 3–5
and then 1 Peter 2 v 19–24

▶ *What was Christ's response to suffering?*

▶ *According to Peter, how should his readers respond to suffering?*

▶ *What in your life do you need to "entrust to him who judges justly"?*

Ask God to enable you to suffer "well" and to follow Jesus' example.

58 – SIMPLY THE BEAST

Job didn't get answers from God about his suffering. He got a new attitude. He realised that what was a puzzle for him to understand was not a puzzle for God. Job knew that not one part of God's creation was outside of God's control.

Read Romans 5 v 6–8

Job, an innocent man, suffered. Jesus,

the perfect eternal Son of God — whose life was far more righteous than Job's — suffered more than anyone. Jesus suffered a cruel human death so that our relationship with God could be restored for ever. Those who live right for God do suffer, but the Bible says no disaster, not even death, can break that restored relationship between God and His people (Romans 8 v 38–39).

59 – HAPPILY EVER AFTER
Read James 5 v 7–11
- ▶ How should we live this life? (v7–8)
- ▶ What shouldn't we do? (v9)
- ▶ How is Job a great example?
- ▶ What does his amazing story show us about God? (v11)

Life here and now isn't all there is. One day, Jesus will return. Christians will go on to something much better. And God will judge those who reject Him. So we shouldn't waste this life judging others and complaining about them. Christians are to be patient, keeping living for God, knowing a perfect life with Him is on the horizon. That means suffering in this life at times. Though probably none of us will suffer as much as Job did. But he didn't turn against God, and the Lord rewarded Him greatly and showed His immense love and compassion.

GALATIANS

61 – NO U-TURN
Read verses 9–10 again
The Galatians had turned back to rules

and rituals. How could they? The Christian life is true freedom. It's not as if our rescue by God hangs in the balance or is in doubt. It's achieved by Jesus' death. It's done. So live like it.
- ▶ Why is special religious stuff (rituals, clothes) so attractive to people?
- ▶ What is it about law-keeping that appeals?

62 – WHERE'S YOUR JOY?
**Read verse 19 again
and then Ephesians 4 v 11–16**
- ▶ Why is Christian teaching so important? (v11–12)
- ▶ What's the ultimate goal? (v13)
- ▶ What do we need to watch out for? (v14)
- ▶ How can we avoid such dangers? (v15)
- ▶ How does the church ("the body of Christ") grow? (v16)

63 – CHILDREN OF PROMISE
Read today's verses again
Today's Bible bit has been a tricky one, but it shows us a great privilege all Christians have. We inherit God's promises from the Old Testament. These promises are no longer fulfilled in the Jewish nation but in Christ and His people — Christians. We are children of promise and citizens of the heavenly Jerusalem — God's kingdom!

64 – DO IT YOURSELF?
Check out verse 7 again
- ▶ Are you running a good race?
- ▶ Are you living in the freedom of knowing you're accepted by God

because of what Jesus has done?
▶ Or are you thinking you're "in" with God by your own achievement?

65 – FREE TO LOVE
Read John 15 v 9–17
▶ How are we to "remain in" Jesus and His love? (v10)
▶ What specific command does Jesus give? (v12)
▶ How did Jesus show His love for us? (v13)

If we love Jesus, we'll obey what He's said. We'll live for Him. Obeying Jesus isn't a boring, annoying chore — it actually gives us joy! (v11) Jesus says: *"Shape up, and follow my example"*. Jesus loves us so much that He gave His life for us. And He expects us to show that same love to other people. Not in a half-hearted way, but being prepared to lay our lives down for other believers.

66 – SPIRITUAL BATTLE
Is there a sin habit you can't seem to kick? Ask yourself these questions:
▶ Do I honestly want to break this sin's hold on me?
▶ Am I trusting God to strengthen me by His Spirit to do that?
▶ Will I resolve daily, with the Holy Spirit's help, to cut that sin out and walk God's way?

67 – FRESH FRUIT
Read verses 22–23 one more time
Why does Paul say "fruit", not "fruits"?

Fruit comes whole, not in pieces. We should be growing in all of these qualities, not just the ones we like the sound of. So the one you spot here that you're least good at is a marker of how you're getting on in each of them.

▶ What steps can you take to co-operate more with God in growing the fruit of the Spirit in your life?

68 – HEAVY WEIGHT
Read Matthew 18 v 15–17
▶ If another Christian wrongs you, what should you do first? (v15)
▶ And if that fails? (v16)
▶ And if that fails? (v17)
Don't rush up to others to retaliate. Our main concern shouldn't be for revenge or getting what's best for ourselves. We should want to help other Christians when they sin, so that they keep living God's way. If you talk over your differences and the other person continues sinning, only then should you bring in other people. We must pray about the situation too.

69 – FIRST-CLASS SERVICE
Check out verse 6 again and then Philippians 4 v 14–20
▶ What had the Philippian church done when Paul was in Thessalonica? (v15–16)
▶ What does v18 say about how God views financial giving? (v18)
▶ These Christians gave generously and sacrificially — how would their needs be met? (v19)

▶ *As Christians give sacrificially and receive what they need from God, what does God receive? (v20)*

PSALMS

71 – LIVING GOD'S WAY

**Read Psalm 119 v 9, 19–22
and then Romans 8 v 1–8**

▶ *What must Christians remember? (v1)*

▶ *What makes this possible? (v2)*

▶ *How does Paul describe people who are ruled by sin? (v5–8)*

▶ *What about people with God's Spirit in their lives? (v5–6)*

If you're a Christian, it should be obvious by the way you live. Your mind is no longer set on doing sinful stuff and it's no longer set against God. Your mind should be set on pleasing God, with the Holy Spirit helping you to live God's way. You're heading for everlasting life and peace with God (v6)!

▶ *Is your life the same as everyone else's?*

▶ *How are you different?*

72 – GOD'S GREAT WORD

The writer of this psalm believes God has planned a path through life for him. And he wants to stick to that route. "Your word is a lamp to my feet and a light for my path" (v105). It may be that following that path will involve suffering, but even that, in God's hands, will be used for God's good purposes. "Before I was afflicted I went astray, but now I obey your word" (v67). "It was good for me to be afflicted so that I might learn your decrees" (v71).

73 – LET'S PRAY

**Read verse 176
and then Isaiah 53 v 4–12**

▶ *What did He have to go through to rescue us? (v5)*

▶ *Did we deserve it? (v6)*

▶ *What did God willingly do? (v10)*

▶ *What would be the outcome? (v11)*

God crushed His own Son. But not because Jesus deserved it — it was the only way to pay for our disgusting sins and our rebellion against God. Jesus was prepared to go through terrible pain, suffering and loneliness for pathetic sinners like us! Incredible.

MALACHI
The big comeback

74 – IN THE END

The Bible clearly explains that God has the ultimate say on who comes to Him and who doesn't. In the end, everything is up to Him. The most important thing for us to grasp is that God invites us to tell everyone about Him (Romans 10 v 14–15). So, even though God plans the outcome of everything, we can be part of His rescue operation, and help people cross over from death to life. God determines the final score, but we still have everything to play for.

75 – BECAUSE I'M WORTH IT

Read Colossians 3 v 22–25

▶ *What's the right attitude to a boss?*
▶ *Why should we do everything "whole-heartedly"?*

Sincere. That's the right attitude to work. And, says Paul, that's how to do "whatever you do". That's worship.

76 – GET OUT!

Read 1 Peter 2 v 9

▶ *What's the job description for the royal priesthood?*
▶ *What other three titles are we given?*
▶ *What three changes have we experienced?*

77 – FAITH BREAKERS

Read Ephesians 5 v 25–33

▶ *What love is a husband to imitate?*
▶ *What is the goal of Christ's love? (v27)*
▶ *What does marriage do to two people? (v31)*

It might not be fashionable, but marriage is amazing! At its heart, two people get to make their lives a picture of the greatest love on earth: Jesus' self-giving passion for His church. Thank God for His undying commitment to His church, and to you as part of it.

78 – FEAR FACTOR

"How can there be a God when the world's in the mess it is?"

▶ *How much of an answer can we give from today's Bible bit?*
▶ *At what point do we have to say that there are things we can't explain and must leave in God's hands?*
▶ *Why should Christians always bring the cross of Jesus into an answer to that question?*

Why not practise your answer on a Christian friend.

79 – GIVING TO GOD

Read verse 10 again

You can't out-give God — He's always more generous. Tithing is an Old Testament principle (Leviticus 27 v 30). But for Christians, giving is a way to thank God for what He gives us.

Check out 2 Corinthians 9 v 6–15, especially v6–7.

▶ *What are the principles for Christian giving?*
▶ *What are you going to do about it?*

81 – PRAY TIME

Read Luke 11 v 1–13

▶ *How are the disciples told to address God? (v2)*
▶ *What are they to pray for first? (v2) What's the reminder in v3?*
▶ *What else is it vital to pray about? (v4)*
▶ *What point is Jesus making in v5–8?*
▶ *So what should we do? (v9–10)*
▶ *What fantastic promise is given to Christians in v11–13?*
▶ *So... how will you change the way you pray?*

82 – CITY DITTY

Read Revelation 21 v 1–4

God will live with His people — in fact

He'll bring heaven down to us! (v2) Heaven and earth will be united: the original relationship between God and humans which existed in the Garden of Eden will be restored. There will be no more sadness or suffering.

PROVERBS

84 – SEX WISE
Read Matthew 5 v 27–30
Adultery in the head is the same as adultery in the bed. So, be ruthless in your attempts to be holy. Ask God for self-control and a desire to please Him.

85 – GREAT ANT
For more proverbs about laziness, check out: **Proverbs 24 v 30–34, 12 v 27, 13 v 4 and 26 v 13–16.**

87 – STRAIGHT THINKING ON SEX
Read Proverbs 7 v 18 again
This is the deception of sexual immorality — the idea that physical romance can satisfy our longing for mutual love and commitment. Sex outside of marriage is ultimately empty and damaging and not the real thing.

88 – WISDOM FOR THE WORLD
Proverbs 8 points forward to Jesus, who is God's Wisdom. The world is complex, but Jesus was the One through whom God created it. So isn't it moronically stupid to think we can live in God's universe without knowing Jesus Christ?

89 – SERIOUS DECISION
Read verses 1–6 again and then Isaiah 55 v 1–7
- Who is God inviting to this amazing feast? (v4–5)
- How should they respond? (v1–2)
- What will coming to the Lord involve? (v6–7)

An amazing banquet has been prepared by God. No money is needed; it's already been paid for. The invited guests only need to accept and come. The "food" that's on offer is actually mercy and forgiveness. Jesus has already paid for it with His life. Best. Invitation. Ever.

90 – SONGS OF ASCENTS
- Do the pressures you face ever tempt you to give up as a Christian?
- What stops you turning to pray to God in difficult times?
- Do you ever think that prayer makes no difference?
- What action will you take to have an attitude more like Psalm 123 v 1?

92 – REST AND REIGN
Read verse 4 again
The Negev was a blazing hot desert that was bone dry during summer and most of the year. But, suddenly in winter, the rains would come and bring the streams back to life. The psalm writer prayed that God would bring life back to His people and restore their fortunes. He was confident that one day God would turn their tears to joy once more (v5).

engage wants to hear from YOU!

- ▶ Share experiences of God at work in your life
- ▶ Any questions you have about the Bible or the Christian life?
- ▶ How can we make *engage* better?

Email us — **martin@thegoodbook.co.uk**

Or send us a letter/postcard/cartoon/cheesecake to: engage, Blenheim House, 1 Blenheim Road, Epsom, Surrey, KT19 9AP, UK

In the next **engage**

Daniel Catch the vision
1 John Sure thing
Ezra Outward bound
Mark True identity
Proverbs Getting God-wise
Plus: Idol worship
Communion & baptism
Do miracles still happen?
Toolbox & Real Lives

Order **engage** now!

Make sure you order the next issue of **engage**. Or even better, grab a one-year subscription to make sure **engage** lands in your hands as soon as it's out.

Call us to order in the UK on 0333 123 0880
International: +44 (0) 20 8942 0880

or visit your friendly neighbourhood website:
UK: www.thegoodbook.co.uk
N America: www.thegoodbook.com
Australia: www.thegoodbook.com.au
New Zealand: www.thegoodbook.co.nz